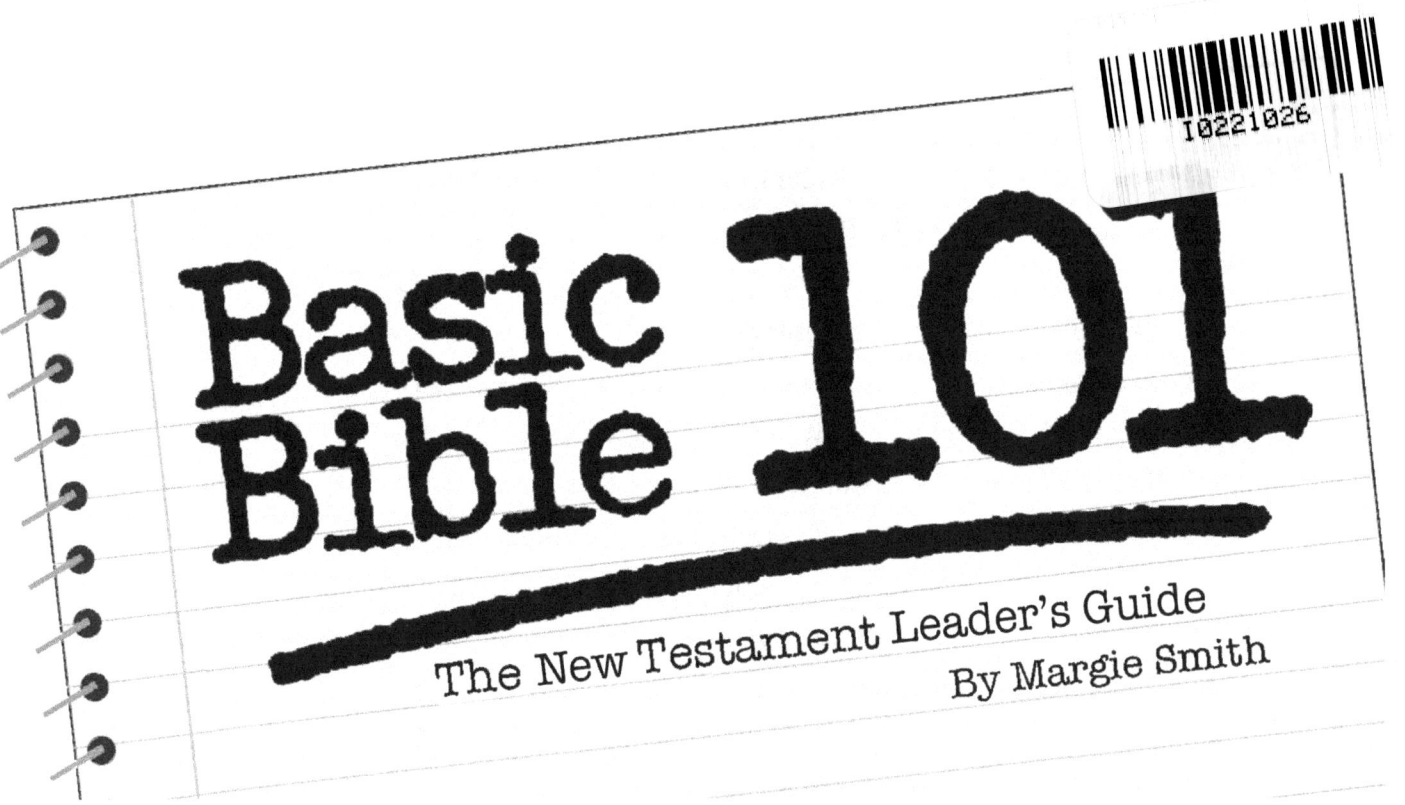

This guide is designed to be used along with the *Basic Bible 101 The New Testament Student Workbook,* and with the podcast of Basic Bible 101 presented by Margie Smith. Reference materials, group leader assistance and answers to the questions posed here are available on line at www.basicbible101.com. Additional information about the author, ordering more books, and accessing the student area of the website can be found on the last page of this guide. Thank you for purchasing *Basic Bible 101 - The New Testament Leader's Guide*.

Copyright @ 2003 Margaret A. Smith All rights reserved. ISBN 978-1-304-95433-6

All scripture quotations, unless otherwise indicated, are taken from The New International Version of the Bible.

Basic Bible 101 - The New Testament
Table of Contents

Lesson 1	What is Basic Bible 101?	1
Lesson 2	The Birth of Jesus	7
Lesson 3	Answering the Call	11
Lesson 4	Jesus' Teachings	15
Lesson 5	The Miracles	18
Lesson 6	The Final Week & Crucifixion	20
Lesson 7	The Resurrection	24
Lesson 8	The Early Church	27
Lesson 9	Paul's Conversion	30
Lesson 10	Paul's Journeys	33
Maps of Paul's Journeys		38
	Paul's Journeys (Continued)	40
Lesson 11	Paul's Letters	44
Lesson 12	The Other Letters	49
Lesson 13	Revelations	52
Quizzes, Final, Assessment Test		56
Back cover: About the Author		

Basic Bible 101 - The New Testament
Lesson 1 - What is Basic Bible 101?

Preparing for the class: *Have all the student notebooks and Bibles ready to pass out. Provide name tags and pens. Greet each student as they arrive. Set out the coffee/juice/snacks or whatever refreshments you decide to serve. Have students fill in the class registration (if applicable) while waiting for the class to begin. Supplemental materials can be found on the website: www.basicbible101.com Encourage previous students to join you for the first session.*

Opening: What is Basic Bible 101?

1. A brief overview of the entire Bible, not an in-depth, verse-by-verse study. There are many ways to explore the Grand Canyon. You can take a backpacking trip down the side, stopping and checking out every little nook and cranny. You can ride the rapids of the Colorado River right through the center, experiencing the thrill, but missing some of the details. Or you can take a helicopter ride over the top, catching a glimpse of things you'd like to go back and explore more fully. This is the helicopter version of studying the Bible.

2. A one year commitment to read the assigned Bible passages, answer the discussion questions, attend every session (as many as you can) and study for the quizzes and finals. You can choose to tackle the larger goal of reading the Bible completely through by following the course outline of recommended readings for that week.

3. An opportunity to:
   • Make friends
   • Share struggles and ask for prayer
   • Learn how to apply the Bible to your present situation
   • Strengthen family relationships

Class Routine: What can you expect each week?

As you can see, you'll have a student workbook, and we'll be using the Student Bible* – primarily so we can all be reading the same words. This class is designed for ***beginner*** students of the Bible, so if you're somewhat familiar with the Bible already you may want to skip this and move into a more challenging Bible study.

We'll begin each week with a review of the previous lesson, then move into a short description of the main story for that day. I'll ask some general discussion questions as we go through the Bible passage, then you'll have an opportunity to share your answers to the discussion questions (homework). Finally, we'll end with a concluding thought and a time for sharing prayer requests.

After we finish a section we'll have a quiz over those lessons, and at the end of the study we'll have a final. If you miss the final you can take it home, but you must return it for class credit. Along the way you'll be given review notes and "pop" quizzes to remind you of the main points.

Instructor Notes:

_____
_____
_____
_____
_____
_____
_____
_____

*Recommended supplemental materials include: *The Student Bible* published by Zondervan, *The Basic Bible 101 Student Workbook,* Basic Bible 101 podcasts and access to the website www.basicbible101.

Lesson 1 - What is Basic Bible 101?

Instructor Notes:

_____
_____
_____
_____
_____
_____
_____
_____
_____

Now, a word from some previous students...

Ask them anything you like. Would any of the Basic Bible graduates here like to say a word about the class?

(Allow about 10 minutes of testimony if former students are available.)

Some Class Rules:

1. You will never be asked to read, pray out loud, answer a question or share anything. You will, however be given an opportunity to do so. I'll simply say, "would anyone like to read ..." I appreciate the help, and I know how hard it is to say some of these Bible names. You'll get more out of the class if you participate, and it will keep people from getting bored with my voice!

2. There are NO stupid questions -- ask whatever you like. If I don't know I'll find out, and if no one knows then we'll just give the various opinions on the matter.

3. The class closes after the 4th week. The reason for this rule is that we will cover so much of the Bible so quickly that it's too hard to make up the missed weeks. If there's enough of a demand we may open another class midway through the year.

Who am I?

(Tell the class a little bit about who you are and why you are teaching the class. Include credentials, testimony, and goals for the class.)

_____
_____
_____
_____
_____
_____
_____
_____
_____
_____
_____

The materials we will be using for this class have been compiled from various sources, but the lessons are from my own personal studying. So, if you disagree with something I've said, and that's OK, I'm totally fine with searching the scripture to discover another way of looking at the discrepancy.

Lesson 1 - What is Basic Bible 101?

What is the Bible?

The Bible is the compilation of the writings from various authors over the course of 4100 years. According to Bible scholars, it begins sometime around 4000 BC with the creation of the world.

The Bible is broken up into two divisions, or Testaments, the old and the new. The word testament means covenant, or agreement – like a marriage covenant (agreement) or "last will and testament". The Bible is all about God's original or Old covenant – agreement – with people, and then God's New covenant that came about with Jesus' death on the cross.

Each testament is made up of books, chapters and verses. Take a minute to thumb through your Bible. Can you find where the New Testament begins? Do you see how each book has several chapters and then the chapters have numbered sentences? The names seem strange to us because they were originally written in Hebrew, the language of the Israel nation. The Old Testament is the basis for the Jewish religion.

How did the Bible get into this form?

The first few Bible stories were passed down from generation to generation simply by word-of-mouth. More than likely it was made into some kind of song or "responsive reading", memorized and re-told on a regular basis. The oldest manuscripts were written on papayas – reeds that were flattened like our paper. The Egyptians used this form of written communication, as well as painting or carving letters on stone. Eventually, the Bible stories were written down, then studied by religious leaders and Bible scholars.

You will notice that most of the books in the Old Testament are narratives, explaining people, places, and events. Some, like Psalms, Proverbs, and the books of the prophets are first person accounts. Most of the New Testament, after the first four books, are letters written to a specific audience. The Jews have studied, memorized and lived by the Old Testament, which they referred to as "the Holy Scriptures." About 285 BC the Old Testament began to be translated into Greek. That version of the scriptures is called the Septuagint, meaning "seventy" because seventy noted Hebrew scholars did the translating.

After Jesus arrived on the scene the disciples wrote the books of the New Testament from first person experience. These books were widely copied in Greek and Hebrew, and circulated during the first two centuries. Non-Jewish Christians went to great lengths to adopt the Old Testament, and began seeing references to the coming Messiah throughout the scriptures. By the third century the church had sophisticated scholars who could defend the Christian claim to the Old Testament by the use of allegory.

Use a poster showing how the Bible came into its present form as a visual aid. Invite students to study it later. You can create one from the lesson or purchase one. See the website for sources.

Instructor Notes:

_____
_____
_____
_____
_____
_____
_____
_____
_____
_____
_____

Lesson 1 - What is Basic Bible 101?

Many people died to bring us this Bible we have.

General distribution began with Gutenberg.

Instructor Notes:

_____
_____
_____
_____
_____
_____
_____
_____
_____
_____
_____

One influential teacher in the early days of Christianity was a priest at Alexandria named Origen, who spoke of the different levels of Scripture.

"The Scriptures were composed through the Spirit of God, and have both a meaning which is obvious, and another which is hidden from most readers… The whole law is spiritual, but the inspired meaning is not recognized by all – only by those who are gifted with the grace of the Holy Spirit in the word of wisdom and knowledge," he wrote.[1]

That's why studying the Bible is so difficult for most people. We can read the words literally, but then we must step back, consider the entire scriptures and listen to the Spirit within us. This way of reflecting on the scripture will help us understand what God is trying to say to us.

Four hundred years after Jesus walked on earth, the Bible as we know, it was first compiled into a single grouping of books. It was translated into Latin by a Catholic priest named Jerome who served under Pope Damasus. This version of the Bible, known as the "Vulgate" is still used by Catholics today. The only real difference between a Catholic Bible and the one we use is the "Apocrypha," 12 or 15 books, depending on how you group them. These books were not originally considered part of the scriptures by Jews in Palestine in the early days of Christianity. Neither Jesus nor the disciples considered them "scripture," but Jews beyond Palestine would include these books in their study of scripture. Christians in the eastern portion of the Roman Empire, nearest Palestine, tended to ignore these books. Western Europe, however, under the influence of Augustine (a well-known bishop of Hippo) accepted these books. In the 16th century during the reformation when the church split, the non-Catholics (Protestants) rejected the Apocrypha.

The books we accept as the New Testament were adopted early in the life of the church and were directly tied to an apostle as a test of the book's validity.

By the 8th century only scholars could understand Latin. So, the only way you could hear God's word was from a priest. In 1383 an Englishman named John Wycliff defied the church authorities and hand wrote an English version of the Bible. Johann Gutenberg, the German inventor of the printing press, printed the first Latin Bible in 1456 but the King and the Church forbid anyone other than a priest to read it. William Tyndale, an Oxford scholar, took Wycliff's version, went back to the original Greek and Hebrew versions, and came up with an English translation of the New Testament in 1525. He smuggling printed copies into England. Tyndale and his editor, John Rogers, were executed for translating the Bible into everyday language.

Lesson 1 - What is Basic Bible 101?

At about the same time Martin Luther, studying to be a priest in Germany, decided that the Bible should be accessible to everyone. He produced a German translation for the common people, which made the Church very upset. His translation was based on the original Hebrew and Greek texts, not the Catholic Vulgate. He was excommunicated from the church (kicked out) and thus began the formation of the Protestant branch of Christianity (i.e. Lutherans, Presbyterians, Baptists, Methodists, etc.).

In 1604 England's King James I called a conference called which included 54 scholars, all experts in Hebrew and Greek. The King commissioned the development of a new Bible. The scholars returned to the Greek and Hebrew text, trying to keep the beauty and style of the original writers. This version is still used today and is referred to as "The King James Bible."

In 1947 a young boy looking for a lost goat found some ancient scrolls in a cave above the Dead Sea in Israel. These scrolls contained the oldest known manuscripts of the Hebrew scriptures, dated about 100 BC. Modern translations reflect some of the newly discovered text.

If you compare all the versions you won't notice a lot of differences. Some are just easier to read than others. We don't use the same language as they did back in England in the 16th century so our modern translations use words more familiar to us. Because we want to be able to follow along when someone else is reading, we will all use the *New International Version* (which is what the *Student Bible* is built around). Whether you use the *Women's Bible*, or *The Journey* or whatever, the primary differences are just cosmetic – side references, little devotion call outs, charts and maps, etc. Other actual Bible translations are: *Good News for Modern Man (GNMM)*, the *Revised Standard Version*, and the *New American Standard*.

The difference between an actual translation and a paraphrase, for example *The Living Bible* or *The Message*, is that a paraphrase is someone's interpretation of the Bible. They are easy to read, and insightful, but don't memorize them. Stick to actual translations for serious Bible study. You may someday write your own paraphrase based on your interpretation of the Bible.

Some Bible teachers prefer one translation over another because of the way some words are translated, but we'll save this discussion for when you are more familiar with Bible content and ready to do more in-depth Bible study. If you would like more information about how the Bible came into being just do an Internet search and you'll find various sources that track Bible translations *(see Wikipedia.org or the International Bible Society website)*.

Martin Luther was cast out of the church for producing a common man's Bible.

The King James conference of scholars.

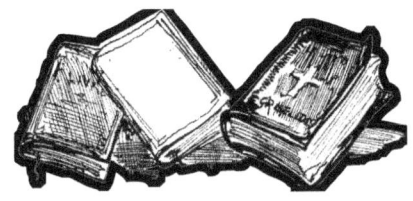

Many translations, but one message.

Instructor Notes:

_____
_____
_____
_____
_____
_____
_____
_____
_____
_____
_____
_____

Lesson 1 - What is Basic Bible 101?

Basic Bible 101 New Testament Overview

For the next four months we will be covering the second major division of the Bible – the New Testament. Much of our discussion will center around the promised messiah proclaimed by prophets in the Old Testament. Christians believe this savior is Jesus Christ. In fact, history is measured by reference to his birth (BC "Before Christ" and AD, a Latin abbreviation for Anno Domini or "Year of our Lord"). I encourage you to read through the entire New Testament as we cover the key points. If you have already taken the Basic Bible 101 The Old Testament, then this course will feel very familiar. If not, then we will need to explain some Old Testament references as we go along, but familiarity with the Old Testament is not necessary for this course.

Questions?

For Next Week: Matthew 1-3; Luke 1-2.

Close in prayer.

Instructor Notes:

Basic Bible 101 - The New Testament
Lesson 2 - The Birth of Jesus

Preparing for the class: *Read the accounts of the birth of Christ in all four gospels. Provide name tags and pens again this week. Set out the coffee/juice/snacks or whatever refreshments you decide to serve. Greet each student as they arrive. Have any new students fill in the class registration while waiting for the class to begin.*

Opening: Moving from the Old to the New Testament

Last week we talked a bit about how the Bible came to be. In today's lesson we will briefly review the Old Testament and then begin the New Testament. For those of you who took the Old Testament Basic Bible 101 class you'll remember we left off with 400 years of silence while the Jews awaited the promised messiah.

The Bridge between the Old and New Testament

When we left the Israelites they were slowly returning from captivity. The proud nation that had once been ruled by King David, King Solomon, and many other good and bad kings, had been destroyed – first by the Syrians and then by the Babylonians. In 586 BC King Nebuchadnezzar II of Babylon conquered the all of Judah and exiled the Israelites to Babylon. In 538 BC Persia conquered Babylon and allowed the captives to return home to rebuild their cities. Just as Israel was beginning to gain some stability the Greek conqueror Alexander the Great swept through all of Persia.

By 333 BC all of Persia was under Alexander's control. It was at this time that the Hebrew scriptures were translated into Greek. This version of the Old Testament was called the Septuagint. At his death all the land that Alexander controlled was divided up between four of his generals. Judah was under the control of Ptolemy I. Conflict began when the king of Syria, Antiochus Epiphanes, seized Palestine.[2] The Jews eventually revolted under the leadership of the Maccabees family. The Maccabees founded the Hasmonean royal dynasty and established Jewish independence in the Hasmonean Kingdom for about one hundred years, from 164 BC to 63 BC.[3] In 63BC Rome gained possession of Palestine. This is where we pick up the New Testament with all of Israel under Roman control.

The Promised Messiah

Under heavy Roman oppression, the Jews began looking for the promised Messiah. Let's look at some of the prophesies that described this coming messiah.

Micah 5:2 "But you, Bethlehem Ephrathah, though you are small among the clans of Judah, out of you will come for me one who will be ruler over Israel, whose origins are from of old from ancient times."

Instructor Notes:

---

[2] *What the Bible is All About, by Henrietta C. Mears, (Regal Books, 1966) p. 333*

[3] *Maccabees. (2009, May 20). In Wikipedia, The Free Encyclopedia. Retrieved 18:00, May 27, 2009, from http://en.wikipedia.org/w/index.php?title=Maccabees&oldid=291288680*

Lesson 2 - The Birth of Jesus

Malachi 3:1 "'See, I will send my messenger, who will prepare the way before me. Then suddenly the Lord you are seeking will come to his temple; the messenger of the covenant, who you desire, will come,' says the Lord almighty."

Isaiah 9:6 "For to us a child is born, to us a son is given, and the government will be on his shoulders. And he will be called Wonderful Counselor, Mighty God, Everlasting Father, Prince of Peace. Of the increase of his government and peace there will be no end. He will reign on David's throne and over his kingdom, establishing and upholding it with justice and righteousness from that time on and forever."

Isaiah 7:14 "Therefore the Lord himself will give you a sign: The virgin will be with child and will give birth to a son, and will call him Emmanuel"

Isaiah 40:3 "A voice of one calling: 'In the desert prepare the way for the Lord'; make straight in the wilderness a highway for our God."

Prophesy Fulfilled
Now let's look at what actually happened. The first four books of the New Testament are called "The Gospels." All four basically tell the same story, the story of Jesus, but from different perspectives. Over the next few weeks try to read all four gospels. We will move back and forth between them considering the story of Jesus in a chronological manner. Turn to the third book of the New Testament, the book of Luke. The Student Bible is filled with all sorts of little study aids. Here you see an introduction to the book. Each book has a similar introduction. That's not part of the actual scriptures, but is added by the editors of this particular version of the Bible. You'll also see some study aids like this part in blue "How to Read Luke." You can use these helpers when you study the Bible on your own.

Read: Luke 1:1-4

Ask: Why is Luke writing this book? (to help Theophilus understand an orderly account of what happened)

Luke goes on to explain that a man named Zechariah, who was a priest in Israel at the time of King Herod, had a strange thing happen when he was serving in the temple. An angel appeared to him and told him his wife was going to have a baby. Now Zechariah's wife had been infertile for many years. So, Zechariah asked how he could be sure of this and the angle said "I am Gabriel, send by God… Now you'll be silent until the baby is born." And with that Zechariah couldn't utter another word.

Read: Luke 1:26-38

Instructor Notes:

Lesson 2 - The Birth of Jesus

As you can see, Mary was surprised by the angel, but her response was a bit different than Zechariah's. She didn't doubt the angel's words. Matthew tells us that an angel also visited her fiancé, Joseph, who knew that there was no way Mary could be pregnant unless there was some foul play somewhere. He believed the angel, and took Mary as his wife. Sometime later Mary went to visit her cousin Elizabeth. Elizabeth confirms the identity of the unborn child in verse 43. Shortly thereafter Elizabeth gives birth to a boy, John, who we'll learn more about in just a minute.

Read: Luke 2:1-20

Discussion groups: (Turn over the groups to the discussion leaders who will review the homework). After about 10 minutes reconvene. Matthew adds the account of the three wise men we see in Nativity scenes. Turn back to Matthew for a moment.

Read: Matt. 2:1-12

Ask: Why do you think King Herod was so interested in where the child was? (he saw the child as a threat to his kingdom and planned to kill him).

Joseph is warned in a dream to take the child and flee to Egypt. After two years King Herod died and an angel told Joseph to return to Israel. Joseph settled in the northern part of the land in Nazareth. (See a map of Palestine during Jesus' life for the exact location).

Luke explains how Jesus was presented in the temple when he was only 8 days old, and two of the servants who worked there proclaimed that this child was the promised one. When he was 12 years old his parents traveled to Jerusalem for the Passover festival, and ended up losing Jesus! They found him speaking with the teachers in the temple, asking questions and impressing them with his understanding of spiritual things. This is about all we know of Jesus' childhood.

Ask: So, whatever happened to Elizabeth's baby, who's he? (John the Baptist)

John the Baptist
Matthew 3 tells us that John grew up and lived in the wilderness, preaching "Repent, for the kingdom of God is at hand." Remember the prophesy about the messenger who would prepare the way? That's John. As he preached people came and he baptized them by dunking them in the Jordan river. Notice the reference in verse 7 to the religious leaders of the day. Many Pharisees and Sadducees were coming to John to be baptized. We'll learn more about these folks next week. John calls them a "brood of vipers." He warns them that after him will come one whose sandals even he is not fit to carry. Al-

Instructor Notes:

Lesson 2 - The Birth of Jesus

though John baptized with water, the coming one would baptize with the Holy Spirit and with fire.

Sure enough, one day Jesus of Nazareth comes to John and asks to be baptized. John refuses at first, saying it is Jesus who should baptize him. But, Jesus insists that this is the right thing to do to fulfill all righteousness. That's why today we continue the practice of baptism when someone becomes a believer in Jesus Christ. Look at verse 16. When Jesus comes up out of the water, the Holy Spirit descends in the form of a dove and a loud voice proclaims, *"This is my Son, whom I love, with him I am well pleased."*

Conclusion:
1. Jesus was born to a virgin, in Bethlehem, was taken to Egypt for awhile to escape King Herod, then returned to Nazareth and grew up like an ordinary boy.
2. Many of the events in Jesus' life were foretold by Old Testament prophets over 400 years earlier.
3. John the Baptist was Jesus' cousin, and recognized Jesus as the Messiah.
4. Jesus is baptized by John the Baptist and a voice from heaven declares Jesus is God's son.

Questions?

For Next Week:
Next week we will see how Jesus begins his ministry, the call of his first followers and some of the things that made Jesus different. In preparation you can read Matthew 4-18, Mark 1-9, Luke 4-9, and John 2-6, or just read Luke 4:1-13 and 5:1-11 and answer the homework questions.

Prayer Requests. Close in prayer.

Instructor Notes:

Basic Bible 101 - The New Testament
Lesson 3 - Answering the Call

Preparing for the class: *Read Matthew 4-18, Mark 1-9, Luke 4-9, and John 2-6. Provide name tags and pens again this week. Have any new students fill in the class registration as they arrive. Set out the coffee/juice/snacks or whatever refreshments you decide to serve. Greet each student as they arrive.*

Opening:
Last week we saw the amazing circumstances surrounding Jesus' birth. We were introduced to John the Baptist and discovered that John was pretty disgusted at the religious leaders of the day. When Jesus came to John to be baptized, John nearly refused, until Jesus explained that it was necessary to fulfill all righteousness. Immediately after his baptism Jesus headed out to the wilderness.

Read: Luke 4:1-13

Ask: Who is the devil? What does he look like?

The devil was originally an angel who rebelled against God (2 Pet. 2:4, Jude 6, Is. 14:12-15). He is first named in Job 1 as an enemy of God. Here we see him trying to persuade Jesus to abandon the purpose for which he came to earth. Notice the first offer Satan presents to Jesus in verse 3.

Ask: Why would food be such a strong temptation for Jesus? (He hadn't eaten for 40 days)

Those of you who have read the Genesis account of Adam and Eve will remember that Eve was tempted with food. The physical body is vulnerable. Sometimes that temptation comes in the form of sexual sin, or laziness, or drunkenness. We live in the real world with real instincts and fears. And we love pleasure – the more the better. It is natural to face temptation on a daily basis.

Ask: Is it a sin to be tempted? (No, Jesus lived a sinless life, yet was tempted. James says that we should consider it a good thing when we face trials and temptations)

Read: James 1:13-17

Ask: Can you see how giving in to temptation results in sin, and sin results in death? What was the second offer Satan made to Jesus? (All the kingdoms of the earth).

Ask: Why would this appeal to Jesus? (The easy way to usher in his kingdom. He will face this same temptation many times through Peter, Judas and the praise of the crowd. Some day every knee will bow to Jesus, the king, but not yet.)

It's not uncommon for us to face the temptation that "the end justifies the means." Sometimes when we know where we're going, when

Instructor Notes:

Lesson 3 - Answering the Call

God has given us a peek at the future, we want to rush to accomplish it through our own means. This temptation is also seen in self-sufficiency (I don't need anyone), in pride (I did it my way) and in get-rich-quick attitudes (I won't need to pay the price). Jesus knew the price he would have to pay. There was no short cut. At his moment of weakness he resisted the temptation to do it his way.

Ask: What was the third temptation offered by Satan? (Prove you're the son of God) How did Jesus answer? (with scripture).

With every attack by Satan, Jesus responds with scripture. What a great idea! Let's see, if we know what God's word says we're better prepared to face the ultimate Liar. Satan has hit Jesus again in a very vulnerable spot – self-identity. Isn't that something we all face? At the beginning of his ministry Jesus had to answer the question, "Who am I?" and "Why am I here?" His time alone in the wilderness with God helped him process these very important questions. We don't know what God said to Jesus those 40 days, but you can be sure Jesus had been preparing all his life for the purpose that God had for him.

How easy it would have been for Jesus to show off. To prove once and for all that he was the son of God. Give up now Satan! You lose. But Jesus knows it's not yet time to reveal who he is to the world. In fact, whenever he does a miracle he tells those around him not to let anyone know about it. Jesus would cause enough commotion without drawing attention to his true identity.

The point of this passage is that temptation is real, it's inevitable and it's very strong. You cannot face temptation on your own – that is why it's so important to get God's word into your head.

Instructor Notes:

Read: James 4:7-10

Ask: How can we resist the power of temptation? (draw near to God, stay pure, humble ourselves before God and he will lift us up).

Calling the First Disciples

One of Jesus' first miracles is found in the book of John chapter 2. Jesus is at a wedding with his family. Apparently a lot more guests showed up for the wedding than were originally expected. Mary, Jesus' mother, comes to him and explains that they've run out of wine. Jesus says "Dear woman, why do you involve me? It's not my time yet," but Mary simply tells the servants standing by to do whatever he says. He directs them to go fill 6 jars with water. Then he tells the servant to draw some out and take it to the master of the banquet. The water has been turned to wine, and not just any wine – the best wine!

People begin realizing that Jesus was different. That Sabbath, the Jews celebrate Friday night to Saturday night as a holy time, Jesus stood in the synagogue in Nazareth, read some of the scripture that pertained to the coming messiah, then explained what it meant. The people were astonished, and skeptical. Wasn't he just Joseph's son? Because of their disbelief Jesus headed out of town. Along the way he found some who did believe in him. Let's look at those who believed.

Read: Luke 5:1-11

Similar experiences happened with other people called by Jesus. In Matthew Jesus calls two brothers, James and John. The book of John describes his encounter with Philip and Nathanael (John 1:43). For the complete list of the 12 disciples turn to Luke 6;12-16. It's a good idea to remember these names (hint: you'll see them again on the final). The interesting thing in all these cases is that when Jesus called people to follow him they left everything and followed.

Ask: Why were these men willing to leave everything to follow Jesus? (Because Jesus had something they wanted. He seemed to know God.) Think about it – why did you follow Christ (if you have)? Why are you checking him out now (if you haven't yet followed him)?

Jesus Sees Us As Individuals

John 4 speaks of his encounter with a woman of questionable morals. He simply asks her for a drink of water, but she is stunned that he would even notice her. He proceeds to tell her details about her life that only she knew. When the disciples return they reprimand the woman for approaching Jesus. Let's look at this story now.

Read: John 4:1-27 (Ask for a volunteer, or several, to help with the reading or just tell the story)

The Samaritans were considered religious outcasts by the Jews. Those of you who took the Old Testament class may remember when Israel became a divided nation and Jeroboam, the king of northern Israel, encouraged the people not to travel to Jerusalem to worship but to worship instead in the hills of Samaria. From then on Samaritans were considered infidels and not true worshippers of Jehovah. They were treated like a Gentile (heathen). Jews wouldn't eat with them, worship with them or allow them in their homes.

Ask: Why was it so upsetting to the disciples to find Jesus speaking to a "tainted" Samaritan woman? (it was socially unacceptable for a Jew to speak to a Samaritan, let alone a woman)

Jesus was an unusual man, willing to cross cultural and social barriers to bring people back to God.

Jesus Begins to Preach Around Galilee

As Jesus draws more of a crowd, the people are mesmerized by his

---

Lesson 3 - Answering the Call

Note to leaders: *If you have time read parts of the story in John 4, but if not just paraphrase the story and encourage your students to read it for themselves.*

Instructor Notes:

Lesson 3 - Answering the Call

words. He speaks with the authority of one who really knows God. Next week we're going to consider some of his teachings.

Conclusion:
1. Jesus was an unusual man, able to withstand temptation, do miracles and cross cultural barriers.
2. When Jesus called someone to be his disciple he gave up everything to follow Christ.
3. As word spread about Jesus people came to check him out.
4. Reactions toward Jesus varied greatly.

For Next Week:
For next week read whatever you didn't cover last week. Read the Sermon on the Mount in Matthew 5-7. If you have time read Mark 4, Luke 6, 8 & 15. Answer the homework questions.

Questions? Close in prayer.

Instructor Notes:

Basic Bible 101 - The New Testament
Lesson 4 - Jesus' Teachings

Preparing for the class: *Read the assigned scriptures. Since the class closes after the third week ask any new students to wait and take the next class, or they can "make up" classes by listening to the podcasts. Set out the coffee/juice/snacks or whatever refreshments you decide to serve. Greet each student as they arrive.*

Opening:
Last week we saw how Jesus faced temptation and how he drew people to himself. The early rumblings about Jesus indicated that many thought he was a prophet. An Old Testament prophet was someone who spoke to the people with God's authority. Many times they weren't welcomed because of the negative things they would say. Jesus, on the other hand, spoke of God as a loving father, someone we'd like to know. He was approachable and wise. Today we're going to look at some of his teachings.

The Beatitudes
One day a group of people were following Jesus around, so Jesus went up on a mountain side and began to instruct them. Let's look at what he said.

Read: Matt. 5:1-12

Ask: What does "blessed" mean? (happy, lucky, joyful)

Most of the crowd were the poor, the meek, the lowly. Jesus spoke kindly to them, not harshly or with condemnation. His words were filled with promise. The hope that someday all the ills of this world would be healed, and the kingdom of God would replace this present oppression sounded just great to these folks. Skip down to verse 17.

Read: Matt. 5:17-20

Ask: Who were the Pharisees and teachers of the law? (The super-religious)

The Pharisees were highly-devoted Jews. They were so sanctimonious that they had their own rule book which included such rules as only walking so many steps on a Sunday. The "teachers of the law", the priests at this time, were equally as self-absorbed, caring more about themselves than meeting the needs of the people. They set up side businesses, such as selling sacrificial lambs, which burdened the common man with high tariffs just to get right with God.

Ask: Was Jesus rejecting their current religion? (No, he came to fulfill the law, not do away with it).

If you look through the end of this chapter Jesus touches on many of the rules that were strictly observed by the Pharisees. See how Jesus takes each law and enhances it? Look at his teaching on murder.

Instructor Notes:

Lesson 4 - Jesus' Teachings

Read: Matt. 5:22

Now, I don't suppose any of you have ever uttered "You Fool" when someone cut in front of you on the freeway, but I've done that a time or two. According to Jesus I would be as guilty as a murderer. Skip down to verse 38.

Read: Matt. 5:38

An eye for an eye, right? Isn't that what we've always heard? But Jesus says turn the other cheek. If someone sues you, give them the money. Don't turn away someone who wants to borrow from you.

Read: Matt 5:43

Love your enemies? Ok, this has gone too far!! No wonder the Pharisees were getting so upset at Jesus.

Ask: How many of you can live by these laws? So what was the point of Jesus raising the standards? They were already so high even the Pharisees could barely keep up with them. (to show that no one could be "good enough" for God to forgive their sins)

As wonderful as Jesus sounded, his message was difficult to understand. This infuriated the Pharisees, the self-professed experts on all things regarding religion, but the crowds must have enjoyed watching the prideful Pharisees squirm a bit. To reach the crowds Jesus told stories. These stories, or parables as we refer to them, usually had an underlying truth. His message was wrapped up in the meaning behind the story. For your homework you read the parable of the Prodigal Son. Take a few minute now to discuss it with your group leader.

Discussion groups: (Turn over the groups to the discussion leaders) 15 minutes. Regroup.

Ask: If you had time to read through some of the other parables Jesus taught, which one did you find the most compelling? (allow time for several responses or if none are forthcoming then share a few that really speak to you.)

I hope we've shed some light on the mystery of Jesus' teachings. No wonder people followed him – you never knew what he'd say! But the crowds not only followed because Jesus was entertaining, he was also able to heal. Next week we'll look at the miracles Jesus did.

Instructor Notes:

Lesson 4 - Jesus' Teachings

Conclusion:
1. Jesus taught with authority, as if God himself was teaching.
2. Jesus taught in parables so that the people could relate to him.
3. Jesus' teachings were controversial and caused many to criticize him and question his credentials to teach.

Questions?

For Next Week:
For next week continue reading through the gospels. Read Matthew 8-10, Mark 7-9 and Luke 7 & 9-19. Or, just read mark 6:30-44 and Matthew 17:1-13. Answer the homework questions.

Close in prayer.

Note to Leaders: An excellent resource for maps, charts and other interesting information is "Nelson's Complete Book of Bible Maps and Charts", by Thomas Nelson Publishers. (A link to this can be found on the Basic Bible 101 website.) This book includes a chart comparing stories found in more than one gospel, which will help your students see the similarities and differences between them. Additionally, a list of all the parables Jesus told will aid your students in finding a particular parable for future reference. Maps can be reproduced for classroom use.

Instructor Notes:

_____
_____
_____
_____
_____
_____
_____
_____
_____
_____
_____

Basic Bible 101 - The New Testament
Lesson 5 - The Miracles

Preparing for the class: *In today's lesson we will look as some of the miracles Jesus performed, and how his rising popularity threatened those in authority. He reveals who he really is to James, John and Peter in the Transfiguration. Finally, Jesus performs the ultimate miracle, raising Lazarus from the dead. Then he heads toward Jerusalem for his final days on earth. As always, set out the coffee/juice/snacks or whatever refreshments you decide to serve. Greet each student as they arrive.*

Opening:
Last week we sat at Jesus' feet, hearing his compelling messages and finding hope in his words. This week we will begin to see the supernatural side of Jesus.

Read: Matt. 8:1-4

Leprosy was a horrible disease that resulted in skin basically falling off the bone. Anyone who had this terribly contagious disease was forced to live outside the city, either alone or with other lepers. When this leper cried to Jesus for help Jesus touched him (that act alone probably appalled the crowd around him) and the man was healed.

Read: Matt. 8:14-18

Word spread and soon Jesus became inundated with sick and mentally ill people. So much so that he could rarely escape the crowds. Jesus began to send some of his followers out two-by-two to the surrounding villages empowering them to spread his teachings and heal the sick.

Read: Mark 6:7-13

Now the news about Jesus had spread far and wide. Thousands flocked to hear Jesus teach and experience his healing power.

Discussion groups: (Turn over the groups to the discussion leaders) 15 minutes. Regroup.

In Matthew 17 you read the account of Jesus with his three closest disciples up on the mountain. They are allowed to catch a glimpse of Jesus in his glory. But not everyone is so convinced that Jesus is the Messiah. At one point he heals a man on the Sabbath, bringing the condemnation of the religious leaders down upon him. As his popularity grows so does the opposition against him.

Read: John 8:12-20

Here we see the controversy over who Jesus really was. The Pharisees have a hard time comprehending that Jesus was the son of God.

Instructor Notes:

Lesson 5 - The Miracles

Read: Luke 9:18-21

Ask: When Jesus asks his disciples who they think he is, what do they say? (Peter got it right, he knew Jesus was the Christ)

Raising Lazarus

One day Jesus receives a message that his dear friend Lazarus was very sick, in fact on the verge of death. Instead of rushing to his side Jesus waits several days. Then he tells his disciples it's time to go. They are naturally concerned because Jesus' life had already been threatened in Jerusalem and Lazarus lives just outside Jerusalem in Bethany. When Jesus explains that Lazarus has fallen asleep the disciples counter, "if he's asleep he must be getting better." But Jesus said plainly "Lazarus is dead."

Read: John 11:17-37 (or paraphrase, but refer to the text so those who want to read the account can do so).

Ask: Why did Jesus wait to come to his friend Lazarus? (verse 15 explains he waited so that the disciples would believe)

Ask: How did Mary and Martha react to Jesus once he did arrive? (both are glad to see him, confused but still hopeful that their brother is in heaven.)

Ask: Why did Jesus cry? (his heart goes out to Mary and Martha. He feels their pain.)

In verses 38-44 we see Jesus walk up to the grave site, ask that the stone be rolled away from the cave where Lazarus was buried, pray to the Father, and call out to Lazarus in a loud voice "Lazarus come out!" Sure enough the dead man walked out of the tomb. All are amazed. Jesus had power even over death. This picture of the power of Jesus would be a foreshadowing of his own resurrection.

Conclusion:
1. Jesus wasn't just a good teacher, he was a miracle worker and master over death.
2. At the height of his popularity thousands of people followed Jesus, even though they didn't really understand who he was.
3. Jesus feels our hurts just as if they are his own. He was fully man and can relate to all our troubles, but he was also fully God.

Questions?

For Next Week:
For your homework read the accounts of Jesus' trial and crucifixion in Matt. 21-27, Mark 11-15, Luke 19-23 and/or John 12-19; or just do the homework assignment Luke 22:47-62.

Prayer Requests. Close in prayer.

Instructor Notes:

Basic Bible 101 - The New Testament
Lesson 6 - The Final Week & Crucifixion

Preparing for the class: *In today's lesson the popularity of Jesus changes quickly to condemnation. We will begin with his triumphant entrance into Jerusalem on Palm Sunday (as we now call it). We will follow him through this final week of his life as he chases out the money changers in the temple, teaches in the synagogue and shares one last supper with his disciples. Then we will watch as Jesus endures torture, a mock trial and finally death. Because today's lesson will end on a somber note, remind your students at the beginning of the class that just last week we learned of the power of Jesus over death. "Weeping may endure for a night, but joy comes in the morning" (Psalms 30:5) Set out the coffee/juice/snacks or whatever refreshments you decide to serve. Greet each student as they arrive.*

Opening:
Last week we focused on the miracles that Jesus did. We saw the confusion in both the disciples and in the religious leaders as to whether Jesus really was the long awaited Messiah. Today we will walk with Jesus through his last week on earth. We will see him stand against injustice and confound the religious leaders with his wise teaching. Finally, we will share an intimate moment between Jesus and his disciples, ending with a betrayal by one of his own. Let's begin.

Read: Luke 19:28-40

Each year the Jews celebrated their exodus from slavery (which is covered in the book of Exodus) with a "Passover" feast. Jesus is returning to Jerusalem to celebrate this event with his disciples. As he enters the city people throw down leaves and coats before Jesus, "rolling out the red carpet" and shouting "Hosannah." It is the beginning of his last week before being crucified by the same crowd.

Instructor Notes:

Ask: Can anyone explain "Passover"?

The Jews celebrate Passover by eating a special meal of lamb, unleavened bread and bitter herbs. This meal is to remind them that when the Lord delivered them from the bitterness of slavery they didn't even have time for the bread to rise. Their lives were spared when the "Death Angel" passed by and saw the blood of a sacrificial lamb on the door posts of their home.

Note to Leaders: Spend more time, if possible, explaining the history of Passover, the symbolism, and that Jesus would become the lamb that allows eternal death to pass from us.

Day by Day – The Last Week
Monday: The next morning Jesus entered the courtyard surrounding the temple. All around him were merchants selling sacrificial lambs for the upcoming Passover event. They charged a small fortune, but the people paid it because otherwise they feared their sacrifice would

Lesson 6 - The Final Week and Crucifixion

be deemed unacceptable. Any animal with a spot or blemish was considered cursed and not worthy of sacrifice. After traveling all the way to Jerusalem it's understandable that some of these lambs might have been bruised along the way. Jesus sees the temple merchants taking advantage of these people and is angry. He throws over the money changer tables, scattering coins everywhere. "My house will be a house of prayer," he exclaims, "but you have made it a den of thieves." At this point the religious leaders try to think of a way to kill Jesus, but the people adore him.

Read: Luke 19:45-47

Ask: Was it a sin for Jesus to get angry? (No, we can get angry, but in our anger we must not sin. See Eph. 4:26-27. Note: if you want to spend a little more time on the anger issue look at James 1, 1 Pet. 5:8, 2 Tim. 2:23-26)

Tuesday: Look at chapter 20

Read: Luke 20:1-8

This confrontation is with the Sanhedrin, the chief Jewish political assembly. Rome appointed the head of the Sanhedrin, the Jewish high priest who led the Sanhedrin. Again they try to trick Jesus.

Read: Luke 20:20-26

Can you see how easily it would have been to catch Jesus with this question? If he said no, they shouldn't pay taxes, then he could be brought before the Romans and prosecuted. If he said yes, the people would not agree because they hated paying taxes to Rome. Right after this the Sadducees, a small sect of Judaism that didn't believe in the resurrection of the dead, tried to trick Jesus with a question about marriage. But again, Jesus answers wisely.

Thursday: On Thursday as the disciples are preparing for the Passover dinner Judas has a change of heart about Jesus. He's the disciple that has been given charge over the group's treasury. Apparently he finally realized that Jesus was not going to mount a political and military campaign against the Romans. He sneaks away and meets with the chief priests. They agree to pay him 30 pieces of silver if he will set up the ambush so that they can capture Jesus. That night Jesus gathers his disciples around him to celebrate the Passover, which will become the last supper. As they arrive Jesus disrobes, puts a towel around his waist and begins washing the disciples' feet. When Jesus blesses the bread he explains "this is my body, broken for you." As he raises the glass of wine he explains, "this is the new covenant in my blood, poured out for you." Today when we share communion, or, "the Lord's supper," we're remembering this moment when Jesus predicted his death on our behalf. Communion and baptism

Instructor Notes:

Lesson 6 - The Final Week and Crucifixion

Instructor Notes:

_____
_____
_____
_____
_____
_____
_____
_____
_____
_____

are the two "ordinances" most Christians share, even though the way we observe them may differ. Then Jesus proceeds to explain to his disciples a bit about heaven and his upcoming death.

Read: Luke 20:31-34

Shortly after this Jesus leads his disciples out to a hill just outside of Jerusalem called the Mount of Olives. He asks them to pray with him. As he prays he sweats drops of blood. In anguish he pleads, "Father, if you are willing, take this cup from me; yet not my will, but yours be done." His disciples are sleepy after the big meal, and doze off. Judas had disappeared, but now he reappears with an army. He greets Jesus with a kiss. When the disciples figure out what is happening they jump up and try to stop the soldiers from taking Jesus. Peter grabs a sword and lops off the ear of the chief priest's servant. Jesus calmly picks it up and replaces it good as new.

From this point on the bewildered disciples scatter. The armed guards take Jesus to the Sanhedrin where the chief priest begins firing questions at him. Finally they ask him if he is the Christ, the son of God, and he said "yes." In their eyes the fact that Jesus claimed to be the son of God was blasphemy and they condemn him to death. But the Sanhedrin couldn't really pronounce a death sentence. They had to bring him before the Roman government to make their judgment official.

Read: Luke 22:47-62 (or just let the discussion group leaders do this)

Discussion groups: (Turn over the groups to the discussion leaders) 15 minutes.

The Trial
Early the next morning they bring Jesus to Pilate, the Roman governor. Turn to Mark's account of what happened.

Read: Mark 15:1-15

Luke adds that Pilate discovered Jesus was a Galilean and decided his case fell under Herod's jurisdiction so he sent him to Herod (governor of Galilee and also in Jerusalem at the time). Jesus was silent before Herod and eventually Herod sent him back to Pilate. Finally Pilate found no reason to condemn him to death, but by this time the crowds had turned against Jesus and were calling for his death. The soldiers began mocking Jesus, putting a purple robe on him and a crown made of thorns. They spat on him and beat him. After they had tortured him a while they led him out to be crucified.

Read: John 19:17-42

The Death of Christ

Here we see the painful, humiliating, heart-breaking treatment of the one sent to bring life to people. Most of the disciples are no where to be found, but John, who refers to himself as the "disciple whom Jesus loved," is nearby with Jesus' mother Mary. Jesus asks John to care for her. Crucified between two thieves, Jesus utters his last words, "It is finished." The soldiers pierce his side to guarantee that he is dead. Quickly they remove the body and throw it in a nearby tomb before the sun sets. The tomb is sealed with a large stone, and Roman guards are stationed at the entrance to see that Jesus stays put. Next week we will see that these guards weren't quite up to the task. Jesus reappears, in a new form, and we call that blessed day Easter.

Conclusion:

1. Jesus committed no crime, was guilty of no sin, and gave his life freely even through he could have stopped the whole process at any time.

2. The two main ordinances celebrated today by most Christians are baptism and communion.

3. The Jews today still celebrate the Passover which commemorates the release of God's people from bondage. Christians know that Jesus was the ultimate Passover lamb, who was slain to buy our freedom from sin and eternal death.

Questions?

For Next Week:

For your homework read the accounts of the resurrection in Matt. 28, Mark 16, Luke 24 and/or John 20-21; or just do the homework assignment in John 20.

Close in prayer.

Instructor Notes:

Basic Bible 101 - The New Testament
Lesson 7 - The Resurrection

Preparing for the class: *In today's lesson your students will see the fullness of Christ as it becomes apparent that even the grave could not hold him. The narrative of discovering the empty tomb is slightly different in the various gospels, but rather than focusing on these slight differences, encourage your students to experience the wonder and delight felt by the disciples when they realize Jesus is alive. For the "doubting Thomas" in your group, ask what it would take for them to believe Jesus rose again. Lead your group through the reconciliation process that brings Peter once again into right standing with Jesus. Invite them to accept the free gift of salvation that Jesus purchased for us on the cross. Set out the coffee/juice/snacks or whatever refreshments you decide to serve. Greet each student as they arrive.*

Opening:
When we ended last week Jesus had been crucified on the cross and his body was hastily laid in a borrowed tomb. Matthew records a few other strange happenings when Jesus died.

Read: Matt. 27:53-54

The curtain in the temple separated the "Holy of Holies," the sacred room where only the High Priest could enter once a year, from the outer area where other priests ministered. Outside this area, Jewish men worshipped, and beyond that the women and children worshipped. Finally, in the outer courtyard, non-Jewish people were permitted. Jesus' death bridged the gap between God and man, making it possible for us to come into God's presence.

Read: John 20:1-18

One thing you'll notice in your study of the resurrection is that each of the accounts from that morning are a little different. Matthew, Mark and Luke mention one or more angels stationed at the tomb waiting for the women. John includes this little story from Mary's perspective. As with any major event, everyone has a different take on what exactly happened. (Kennedy assassination, 911, serious auto accident). We do know that the stone covering the tomb was rolled away, the guards were gone and so was Jesus. We know that Jesus appeared to Mary, to two disciples walking along the road to Emmaus outside Jerusalem (perhaps one of these was Luke), and to most of the eleven disciples back in Jerusalem Sunday night. But one of the disciples was not with the group that evening.

Read: John 20:24-31

Take out your homework and work in your group with your discussion leader.

Discussion groups: (Turn over the groups to the discussion leaders) 15 minutes.

Instructor Notes:

Lesson 7 - The Resurrection

The Resurrected Body

Jesus appeared again to his disciples at the Sea of Tiberias. John 21 describes this account of the disciples coming back from fishing and finding a man on the beach who asked if they had any fish. They didn't but he recommended that they throw their net out again. When their net came back full Peter said, "it is the Lord" and jumped out of the boat, rushing to shore to be with Jesus. He fixed them breakfast and ate with them.

Ask: What do you notice about the physical appearance of Jesus? (he eats, they can touch him, he still has wounds, he could be recognized, but not easily) This may give us some clues as to what our resurrected body will be like.

Read: John 21:15-17

Ask: Did you notice how many times Jesus asked "do you love me?" (3)

Ask: Do you think that was significant for Peter? (Since he had denied Christ three times it was a fitting way to empower the man who would become the head of the early church).

The Importance of the Resurrection

The Jews had made up some story about how Jesus' body was stolen after the earthquake. Today some people do not believe that Jesus really came back from the dead. We have talked over all the stories of who Jesus was – some say he was just a great teacher, others a prophet, still others believe he was a god, but not Thee God. Who do you believe he was?

Ask: Why is it important to the Christian faith that we understand and accept the resurrection of Christ? (If Christ wasn't raised from the dead, then he didn't have power over sin and death. If so, then he wasn't who he said he was and we believe a lie.)

Ask: Why did Jesus have to die to forgive our sin? (Only the shed blood of the perfect sacrifice could atone for our sin once and for all.)

Ask: Would anyone like to share what this means to you personally? (Allow a few moments for testimony)

Read: Matt. 28:16-20

Instructor Notes:

Lesson 7 - The Resurrection

We call this passage "The great commission" because here Jesus charges the disciples with sharing the good news with everyone. Forty days later Jesus ascended into heaven and told the disciples to wait in Jerusalem until they received the "power of the holy spirit." We'll find out more about that next week.

Points to remember:
1. Jesus didn't stay dead. He appeared first to Mary, then two disciples, then more of his disciples, then to Thomas, then to many.
2. Because Jesus died for our sins, and conquered even death, we can be confident of God's forgiveness of our sins and eternal life if we believe in him.
3. Jesus' resurrection body was real, touchable and could digest food!
4. Our responsibility as followers of Christ is to "make disciples."

Questions?

For Next Week:
Next week we will discover what happened with these followers of Jesus. For your homework read the accounts of the early church in Acts 1-12, or just read the homework passage, Acts 2 and 9.

Close in prayer.

Instructor Notes:

Basic Bible 101 - The New Testament
Lesson 8 - The Early Church

Preparing for the class: *Set out the coffee/juice/snacks or whatever refreshments you decide to serve. Greet each student as they arrive. Pass out Quiz 1 over the life of Jesus and have the students fill it in while they're getting their refreshments. Go over the answers at the end of class.*

Opening: Last week we covered the resurrection of Jesus. The death & resurrection of Jesus took place around 29 AD. Today we will begin the book of Acts. Acts is thought to have been written by Luke. He's writing this book to Theophilus sometime after he wrote the book of Luke. Luke records the birth and rapid growth of the early church.

Pentecost

Jesus had already told his followers not to leave Jerusalem until the Holy Spirit baptized them. I'm sure they hadn't a clue what that meant. Approximately 50 days after his resurrection the disciples and other new converts are praying when a strange thing happens.

Read: Acts 2:1-13

Ask: Why do you think some of the locals considered them drunk? (They were acting strange, excited, giddy)

In verse 14 Peter addresses the crowd explaining that the believers aren't drunk, they are just filled with the spirit of God. Peter then proceeded to describe who Jesus was, why he came and what to do to become right with God. The Holy Spirit spoke through Peter giving him boldness and clear thinking as he was speaking.

> *Note to Leaders: Questions may arise about "speaking in tongues" and its use today. Because of time constraints try to answer briefly and encourage interested individuals to talk with you or one of the ministers after class.*

Read: Acts 2:36-41

Ask: So, what is the result of Peter's words? (The people are deeply moved and ask what they should do. Peter tells them to repent, ask God for forgiveness and be baptized.)

The Early Church

As we've seen the church grew very fast. Many of the believers were poor, from other parts of the country and/or without family. Even those with family were cast out from their family once they professed Jesus. So the disciples began to encourage everyone to share what they had. Everyone brought food, clothing, money or whatever they could to help their brothers and sisters in Christ.
In verse 42-43 we see that the believers were together nearly all the

Instructor Notes:

Lesson 8 - The Early Church

time. The apostles were able to do miracles, just as Jesus had done, and they began a kind of communal living.

In Chapter 3 John and Peter are heading to the temple and a poor crippled man asks them for a handout. Peter replies, "silver or gold I do not have, but what I have I give to you. In the name of Jesus Christ of Nazareth, walk." The man stands, begins walking around, then starts jumping for joy. Peter uses this opportunity to tell those watching this spectacle about Jesus. When the chief priests heard about this they were greatly disturbed and brought Peter and John in for questioning.

Read: Acts 4:7-22

Ask: Why wouldn't Peter and John just pipe down for a while until the religious leaders had cooled off a bit? (They were filled with the Holy Spirit)

Ask: What does it mean to be "filled with the Spirit"? (Answers may vary)

Because Peter and John didn't stop speaking about Jesus they were jailed. In Chapter 5 verse 29 Peter remarks, "We must obey God rather than men." During the night an angel releases Peter and John from jail and instead of hiding out for a while they return to the temple courts and again begin preaching about Jesus. Peter clearly accuses the crowd of killing Jesus. The apostles are beaten, then released. The climate for Christianity had definitely grown hostile.

Deacons

In Chapter 6 the number of believers has grown so large that the original 12 can't handle all the organizational details so they choose seven men to help out, which are then referred to as deacons. These men help out the widows and orphans by organizing the meals and providing aid. A couple of these names will become familiar. Specifically, Stephen is mentioned in Chapter 7, and Philip in Chapter 8. Stephen becomes the target for those trying to destroy this new religion.

Read: Acts 6:51-60

Stephen the Martyr

In Chapter 7 Stephen gives a great review of the Old Testament, and an account of how he came to believe in Jesus. In the process he said some things that greatly angered the religious leaders, specifically that Jesus was the righteous one, the Son of God, and they murdered him. The accusers are so mad they drag him out of town and begin throwing stones at him. While they are killing him a young man named Saul holds their coats.

Instructor Notes:

Read: Acts 6:54-60

Take out your homework and work in your group with your discussion leader (go over the homework in the large group.)

Discussion groups: (Turn over the groups to the discussion leaders) 15 minutes.

Questions?

Conclusion:
1. *The Holy Spirit is real, and it can change your life.*
2. *Believers become family, that's why we refer to eachother as "brothers and sisters in Christ."*
3. *You may be asked to suffer for your faith.*
4. *The believers scattered because of the persecution of their faith, thus the gospel spread throughout Judea and Samaria.*

Next Week: We will be introduced to Saul and the impact he will have on the early church. Read Acts. 8-20

Close in prayer.

Instructor Notes:
_____
_____
_____
_____
_____
_____
_____
_____
_____
_____
_____
_____

Basic Bible 101 - The New Testament
Lesson 9 - Paul's Conversion

Preparing for the class: *You might begin the lesson by bringing all kinds of bugs, worms or other undesirable things and putting them on a plate with a knife and fork. Read Acts 8 – 20. No snacks today - just bugs. Hang a map of the region that includes Tarsus & Damascus.*

Overview: The church, now under heavy persecution, is forced to go underground. Saul is tracking down believers and having them arrested. Some believers head north to the coastal down of Damascus. Others head inland or south to Egypt. Today's lesson explains how Jesus appeared to Saul, and the dramatic change it made in his life. In this lesson Peter faces the issue of letting Gentiles become part of the fellowship of believers, and Paul begins his journey to share the gospel with other nations. After this lesson your students should be able to tell how Jesus appears to Saul and Saul then becomes Paul. Be prepared to describe the challenge for Peter in accepting Gentiles into the faith. This lesson will also introduce your students to Barnabas and why he was so important to Paul.

Presenting the Lesson: Begin by asking who would like to try one of these delicacies? (referring to the plate of bugs). Today's lesson deals with moving outside our comfort zone. Last week we left off with one dead deacon, Stephen, and one pious young man cheering on the murders. That man was Saul, but after today's lesson we'll refer to him as Paul. Turn to Acts Chapter 8.

Read: Acts 8:1-8

Ask: Why did Saul think he was justified in putting these people in prison? (He was a righteous Jew who thought that Christ's followers were undermining the Jewish religion. He was protecting his faith in a kind of holy war.)

We're going to skip over the rest of Chapter 8. There's an interesting story about a sorcerer who tried to buy the gift of the Holy Spirit. Philip, the deacon, is preaching mightily to the Samaritans, and the Lord sends him to an Ethiopian traveler who also becomes a believer.

Read: Acts 9:1-18

Ask: So, what was "The Way"? (code name for believers of Jesus)

Ask: Why do you think Paul was stricken blind? (to get his attention, slow him down, get him to focus inwardly instead of outwardly, convey the seriousness of what he was up against)

Paul is a very smart, very determined man. He later refers to this experience as his credentials for being an apostle. He felt Jesus' appearance was to him his "call", as though he had been born just a

Instructor Notes:
_____
_____
_____
_____
_____
_____
_____
_____
_____
_____
_____
_____

bit too late. But the other believers are naturally skeptical of Paul's conversion.

Ask: How do you think Ananias felt about going to Paul? (fearful, excited maybe?)

Ask: How does God refer to Paul (see verse 15)? (God's chosen instrument to carry his name before the Gentiles)

Paul began to preach immediately in Damascus, but many were critical of him. They didn't believe he had really converted. He heads out to the wilderness (Gal. 1:17-18) then back to Damascus.

Ask: How do you think the other believers felt about Paul? (Suspicious maybe, bitter. Some may have praised God for his conversion.)

Paul spends time with James in Jerusalem, then in fear for his life travels to Tarsus. Barnabas brings Paul from Tarsus to Antioch, introducing him to the believers and greatly encouraging Paul. It is here in Antioch (show on map) that the believers are first called "Christians." In the mean time the believers back in Jerusalem are getting more organized and beginning to look like a "church." At the end of Chapter 9 Peter raises a woman from the dead. Then in Chapter 10 a strange thing happens to Peter.

Read: Acts 10:9-20

Ask: Why was Peter so appalled at eating "unclean" food? (Up to this point the believers were all still clinging to their Jewish traditions. Jesus was kind of an add-on to their existing beliefs)

Just like we wouldn't eat bugs and worms, Peter has been brought up to believe the food on the sheet was disgusting. What Peter doesn't know is that at the same time a Gentile Centurion (soldier) by the name of Cornelius, in Caesarea (on the coast), had had a strange vision too. In his dream he saw an angel of God call him. The angel said God had noticed his prayers and gifts to the poor. Cornelius was to send for Peter who was now staying with Simon the tanner. When Peter arrived at the house, Cornelius fell at his feet in reverence, but Peter made him get up and said he was only a man not God. A large gathering of people were there, so when Peter began to speak to them he made it clear he was a Jew and Jews didn't associate with Gentiles.

Read: Acts 10:28-29

Obviously God was working in Peter's life. Cornelius proceeded to explain his strange vision, then Peter preached about Jesus and everyone in the house is deeply moved by his words.

Instructor Notes:

Lesson 9 - Paul's Conversion

Read: Acts 10:44-48

Discussion groups: (Turn over the groups to the discussion leaders) 15 minutes. Or cover the homework together.

After Peter shares the Gospel with these Gentiles, and they accept the message of Jesus, Peter is in big trouble with his fellow Jewish believer's back home. Peter related his vision and the experience he had with Cornelius. The Holy Spirit must have been speaking through him because the Jewish believers were convinced. Yes, Jesus came for the Gentiles too. (Aren't you glad he did!!). Just as we are loath to accept anything outside our tradition (for example eating bugs), the new believers could have easily excluded the Gentiles, but Jesus brought salvation to all the lost. Think about some of your hard and fast traditions. Are they keeping you from God's purpose in your life?

Conclusion:
1. *When God gets a hold of you he changes you – to the very core of your being.*
2. *A good friend like Barnabus is a great support in times of trouble.*
3. *Old traditions must die if you're going to be free to serve God – he makes the rules.*

Questions?

Next Week: For next week read through the journeys of Paul, Acts 13 – 28. Along the way Paul writes to many of the people he met, and those letters become books of the New Testament. Spend some time reading 1 and 2 Thessalonians.

Close in prayer.

Instructor Notes:

Basic Bible 101 - The New Testament
Lesson 10 - Paul's Journeys

Preparing for the class: *Read the rest of the book of Acts. Set out the coffee/juice/snacks or whatever refreshments you decide to serve. Set out highlighters for map work. Have extra copies of the "Journeys of Paul" maps available. If possible hang a large map for reference. Greet each student as they arrive.*

Presenting the lesson: Read and review the target scripture carefully, then tell most of the story rather than read it. You may choose to cover this lesson over two sessions to allow more time to discuss the letters Paul wrote along the way. If you do be sure to read the overviews for these books in Lesson 13. Encourage the students to read all of Acts for themselves if they haven't already.

Opening: Last week Saul became Paul when he had a close encounter with Jesus on the road to Damascus. The experience so changed Paul that he immediately began preaching and learning everything he could about Jesus. The believers are skeptical at first, but then accept Paul. Meanwhile Peter had a strange experience with some Gentiles. They, too, received the message of Jesus and believed. The gospel appears unstoppable.

Read: Acts 11:19-26

Paul teams up with Barnabus (his name means "Son of Encouragment") who "disciples" or trains Paul for an entire year in Antioch. In the mean time James, the brother of John, is put to death by King Herod and Peter is arrested.

Read: Acts 12:1-10

Peter Imprisoned
Peter was captured during Holy week just as Jesus was. While he was in prison the disciples were praying. When an angel rescued him Peter didn't know what to think. He decides to head to Mary's house (John Mark's mother). He knocked on the door and the servant girl answered. She was so excited it was Peter that she ran back to tell the others and forgot to unlock the door. Some welcome home! When the guards couldn't find Peter the soldiers who were guarding him were put to death. At the end of chapter 12 King Herod delivers a speech that impresses everyone to the point they call him a god. He is puffed up with pride, but the Lord God will not share his glory with anyone. He curses him and Herod is eaten by worms.

Paul's First Missionary Journey
At this point the church in Antioch felt led by the Spirit to send Paul and Barnabus to preach the gospel throughout Cyprus and into Lycaonia (modern day Turkey). Let's look at their first trip. He begins with a short hop over to Cyprus.

Instructor Notes:

Maps: Trace the route Paul took with your highlighter on his first missionary journey.

Note to Leaders: Point out each city visited by Paul and give a brief description of how they were received.

• They sail to the island of Cyprus, cross the island, to Salamis and called out a false prophet (BarJesus who was feeding lies to the proconsul there). Paul curses BarJesus with blindness.

• Then they sail on to Perga (modern day Turkey). John Mark leaves them and returns home (which irritates Paul).

• They travel north by foot to Pisidian, Antioch, where the local Jews invite them to speak. Paul preaches of how Jesus is the fulfillment of the promised messiah, and can forgive sin. The congregation was intrigued and asked Paul to speak again the next week, but on that day the crowds were so great that local Jews were jealous and denied Paul's claims. They were chased out of town.

• Paul & Barnabus travel to Iconium, again begin speaking in the Jewish temple and many believed. Again the non-believing Jews revolted against then, but the Lord allowed them to do many miraculous signs to confirm the message. The Jews plot to stone them, so they fled to Lystra & Derbe in Lycaonia.

• In Lystra Paul heals a crippled man. The people are so astonished they call him a god and start to worship Paul and Barnabus. Paul of course refuses to be worshipped proclaiming God's plan of redemption for all. Jews from Iconium show up and turn the crowd against them, so much so that Paul is dragged outside the city and stoned. Left for dead, he gets up and returns to the city. He and Barnabus left for Derbe the next morning.

• In Derbe they were well received. They retrace their steps through Lystra, Iconuim and Perga, encouraging the believers along the way, then returned home to Antioch.

As a result of their journey many believed and several new churches began. When they returned they told the Jewish believers at the church back in Jerusalem what had happened. The church council was concerned that the new Gentile believers were not converting to Judiasm, becoming circumcised, practicing Jewish eating regulations, etc. Paul argued on their behalf, convincing the church council that Christ alone was enough to bring about salvation. The council gave a few other suggestions and let it go at that.

Read: Acts 15:21

Ask: How did the early church settle their disagreements? (face to

Instructor Notes:

face, with complete reporting, with much discussion, observing the facts, listening to the Holy Spirit, study of scripture, with deference to grace)

Paul's Second Missionary Journey

Once again Paul set out for another missionary journey, this time through the interior of modern day Turkey and on up into Greece. He had planned to go into Asia, but the Holy Spirit stopped him, so he turned toward Europe. Macedonia (Greece as we know it) was the crossroads of the world at that time. Paul and Barnabus had a disagreement over whether to take John Mark. Paul refused to take him because he deserted them on the last trip.

Beginning in Chapter 16 Paul is traveling with Timothy, Silas, and the author of Acts, which many believe was Luke. Luke writes in first person, describing what happened from his personal experience.

Maps: Trace the route Paul took with your highlighter on his second missionary journey.

• Paul and Silas travel back through Syria strengthening the churches that sprang up after the last missionary journey. This time they take the land route, up through Paul's home town of Tarsus, then on up through Derbe, Lystra, Iconium and Antioch.

• In Lystra he met a young disciple named Timothy, whom he allows to travel with them the rest of the journey.

• They move on up through Galatia, then Paul has a vision of a man asking him to come to Macedonia (modern day Greece) so he turns toward Troas (a seaside city).

• Crossing the Aegean Sea the group travels through Samothrace and on to Neapolis, eventually ending up in Philippi. Here Paul speaks to a group of women down near the river and one of them, Lydia, becomes a believer. She invites them into her home where her entire family is saved. They start a church in her home.

Read: Acts 16:16-24

Ask: What did Paul and Silas do to make the people so mad? (healed a "psychic" girl).

Read: Acts 16:25-40

Ask: Why would the jailer almost kill himself when he thought the prisoners were gone? (His punishment for losing the prisoners would be very painful and disgraceful)

Instructor Notes:

Lesson 10 - Paul's Journeys

Ask: How did the jailer respond to God's grace displayed through Paul and Silas? (he asked, "What must I do to be saved?")

The jailer and all his family became believers.

• Leaving Philippi, Paul and his team passed through Amphipolius and Apollonia to Thessalonica. Here Paul preached in the synagogue for three consecutive weeks. Many believed, but again the jealous Jews found a way to start a riot against them. Paul and his crew were sent away to Berea.

• In Berea the people were open to Paul's message and received it with joy. But when the Thessalonica Jews heard Paul was peaching there they immediately showed up and stirred up the crowds against Paul. The brothers there sent Paul away, but Silas and Timothy stayed on to lead the new believers.

• Paul arrives in Athens, waiting for Silas and Timothy to catch up. While he's here he was greatly troubled when he noticed all the idols in this place. When he stands up to speak he taps into their way of thinking, referring to the idol for the "unknown God."

Read: Acts 17:22-33

Ask: Does Paul's argument of an "unknown God" make sense in light of today's beliefs? (discuss yes or no)

Ask: How did the people respond to his presentation? (some believed, others wanted to hear more later – just like people respond today.)

• Paul leaves Athens and ends up in Corinth. Finding a receptive audience for the gospel, Paul stays for here 18 months working as a tentmaker when he wasn't preaching. Silas and Timothy catch up with him. While there he wrote his letter to the church in Thessalonica, our first book of Thessalonians.

Note to Leaders: You may decide to cover Paul's letter of 1 Thessalonians here, or wait until you've covered all the missionary journeys. An overview of Thessalonians is included in the lesson on Paul's letters.

• In Corinth Paul develops a close friendship with a couple – Priscilla and Aquila – who are also tentmakers. These two travel on with him to Ephesus, then began a new church there. Paul then returns to Jerusalem and then on to Antioch.

Instructor Notes:

Lesson 10 - Paul's Journeys

Conclusion:
1. *The gospel upsets people. You can't share the gospel without eventually encountering resistance.*
2. *One way to reach non-believers is to identify with something they already believe, just as Paul did with the "unknown God" argument.*
3. *Old traditions must die if you're going to be free to serve God – he makes the rules.*

Questions?

Next Week: For next week finish reading the journeys of Paul through the end of Acts, if you haven't already. Spend some time reading the letters of Paul. Start with 1 & 2 Corinthians, Galatians and Romans.

Close in prayer.

Instructor Notes:

_____
_____
_____
_____
_____
_____
_____
_____
_____
_____
_____
_____

Lesson 10 - Paul's Journeys

Paul's First Missionary Journey

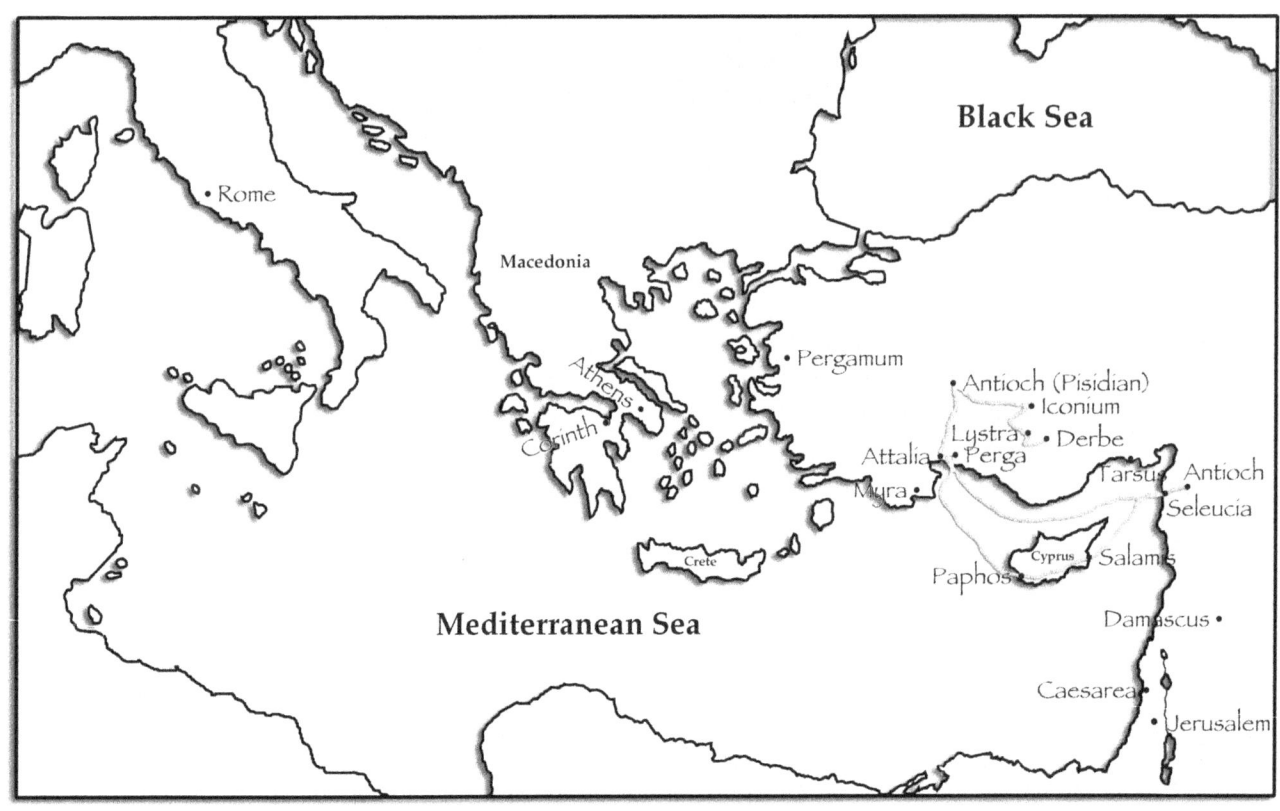

Paul's Second Missionary Journey

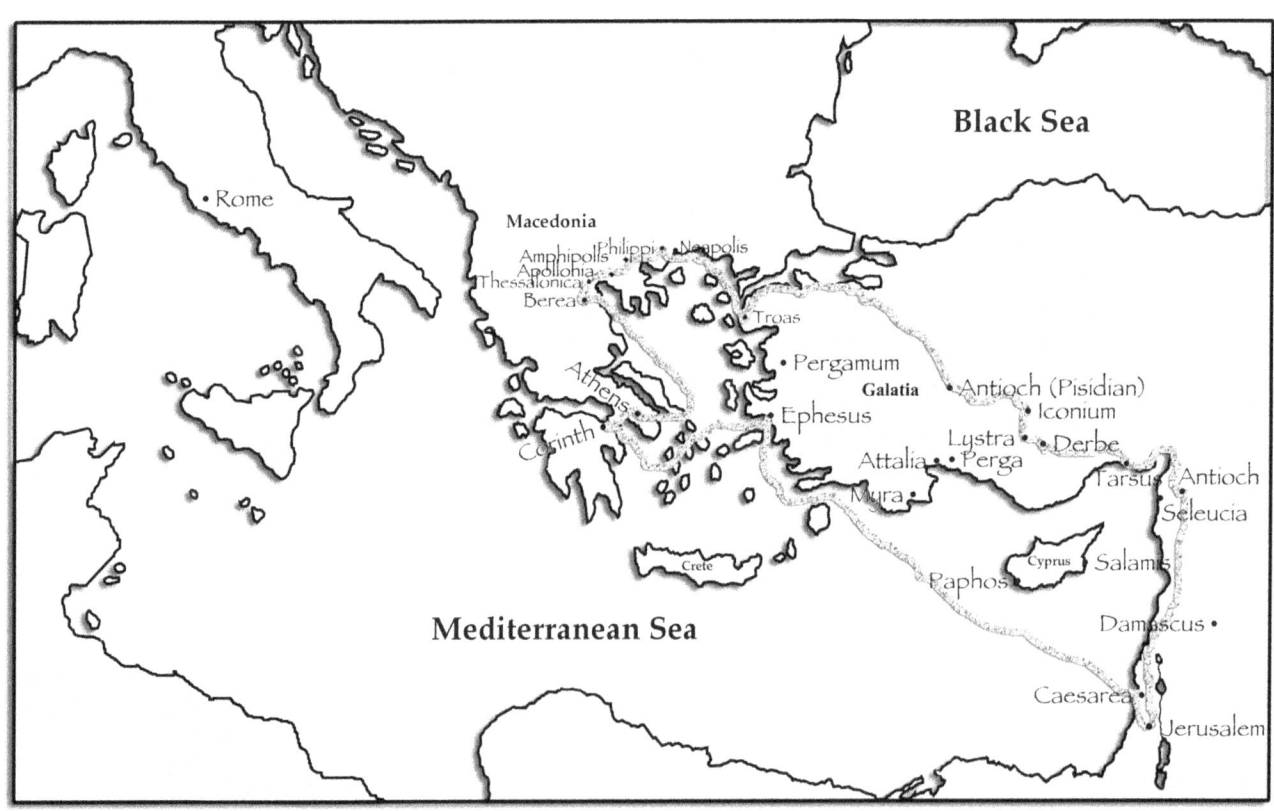

Paul's Third Missionary Journey

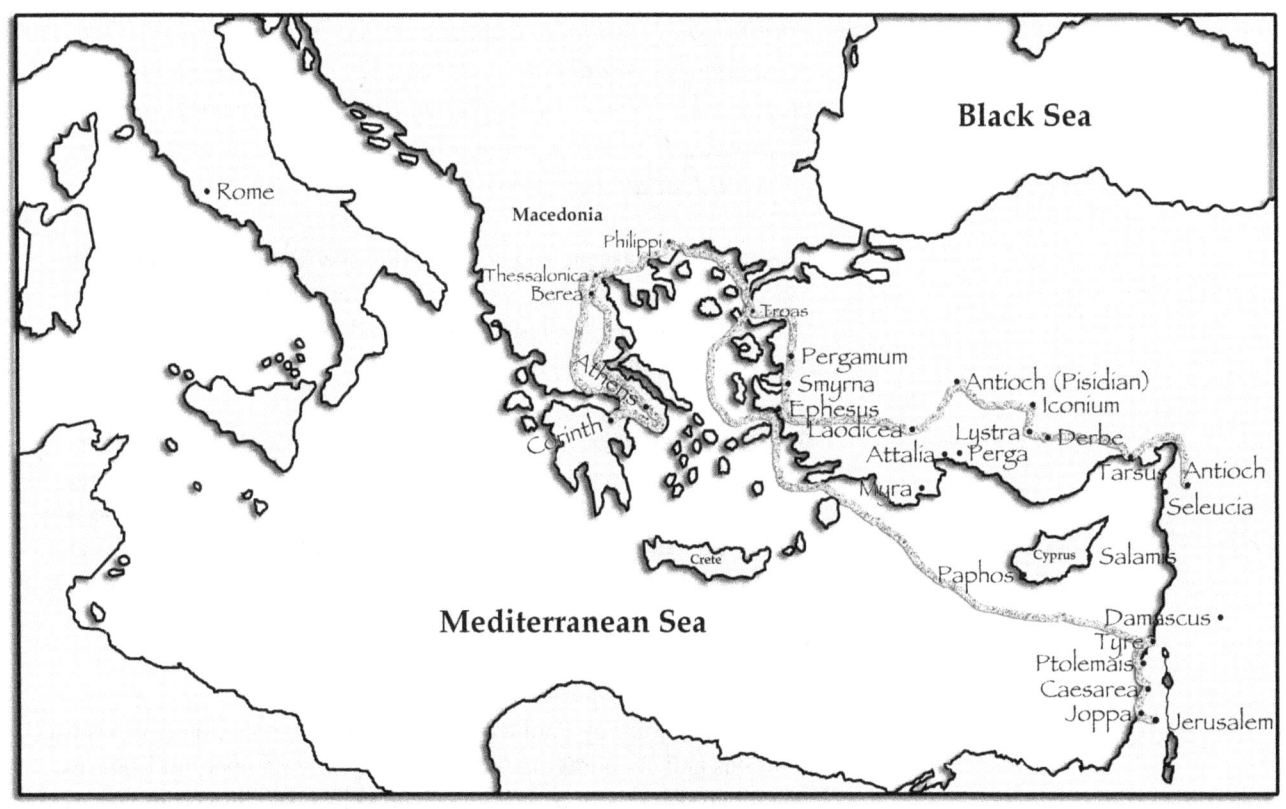

Paul's Journey to Rome

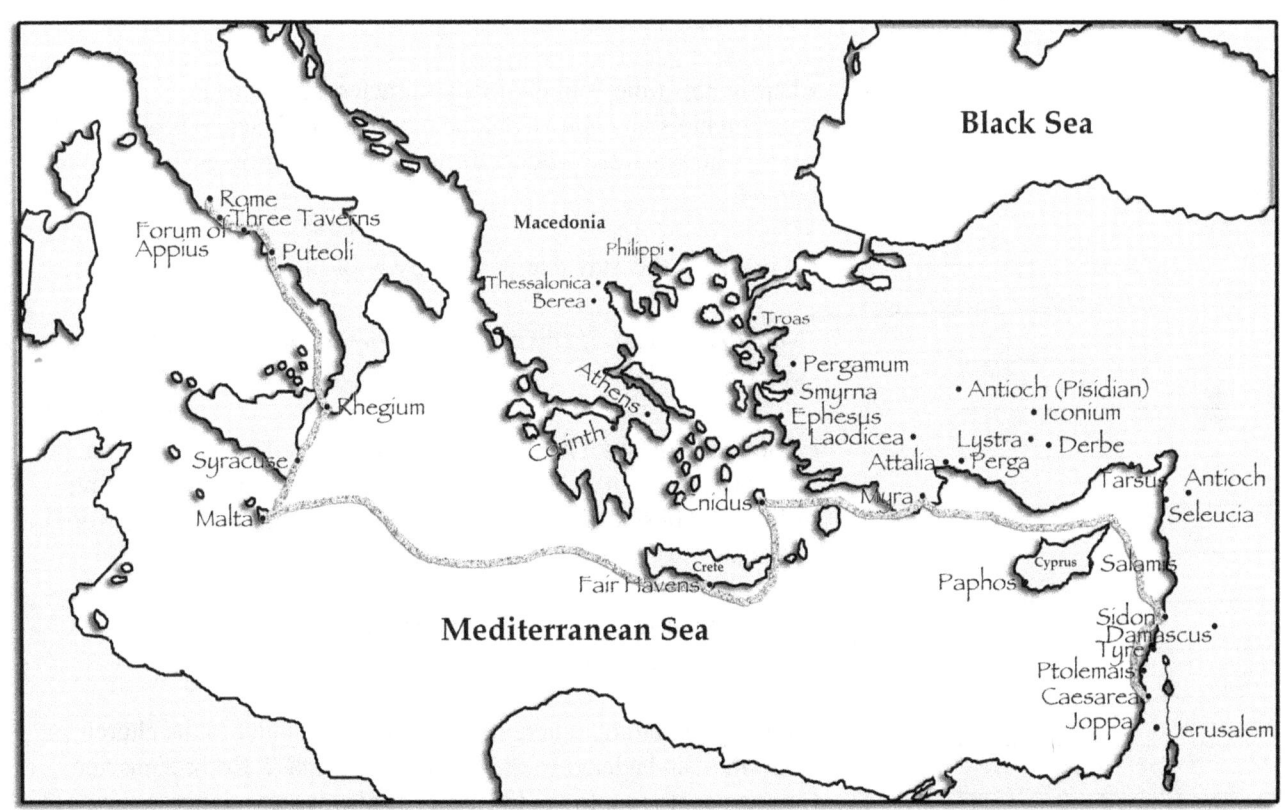

Basic Bible 101 - The New Testament
Lesson 10 - Paul's Journeys (cont.)

Preparing for the class: *Read as many of the letters of Paul as you can. Review the book introductions in the Student Bible or another study Bible. Set out the coffee/juice/snacks or whatever refreshments you decide to serve. Set out highlighters for map work. Have extra copies of the "Journeys of Paul" maps available. If possible hang a large map for reference. Greet each student as they arrive.*

Presenting the lesson: Today you will cover Paul's third and forth journey. If you chose to cover Paul's letters along the way be sure you have reviewed the letters mentioned in this lesson. Read the overviews for those books in Lesson 13.

Opening: Last week we traveled with Paul through Macedonia as he spread the good news. Many new believers accepted the message of Christ and new churches popped up all over Asia. Along the way Paul wrote back to these new believers. Last week we talked about his letter to the Thessalonians. Today we will cover more of Paul's letters while we trace his last two journeys.

Paul's Third Missionary Journey

For his third journey Paul traveled back through the interior, visiting churches and encouraging the believers, arriving again in Ephesus. Some believers there hadn't heard the details of Christ, but were followers of John the Baptist. When they learned about Jesus they believed. One of these converts, Apollos was sent on to Corinth to teach there.

• During this time Paul did many miracles, so that even handkerchiefs and aprons that he touched were used to heal the sick. Many who practiced witchcraft turned over their magic books to be burned.

• It is during this stay that Paul likely wrote 1 Corinthians.

Note to Leaders: If you decided to cover Paul's letters along the way, stop and review 1 & 2 Corinthians and Galatians.

• While in Ephesus a huge riot broke out, started primarily by an idol maker (silversmith) who was worried that with so many believing in Jesus his business would suffer. Shortly thereafter Paul left for Greece.

• Paul remained in Greece for three months encouraging the new churches along the way.

• Somewhere along in here he wrote a second letter to the church in Corinth, and a letter to the church in Galatia (2 Corinthians and Galatians). Hoping to get to Rome, he also writes a letter to the

Instructor Notes:

Lesson 10 - Paul's Journeys (cont.)

believers there (Romans).

• Paul travels back through Phillipi and meets up with the rest of his team at Troas.

• Paul's journeys are successful. So successful in fact that people crowd into houses to hear him speak. In one incident at Troas Paul is preaching late into the night and a young man sitting on a window ledge nods off to sleep and falls out the window and dies! (Act. 20:7-12). Paul threw himself on the man and he comes back to life. (Who does this sound like? Elisha)

Completing his third missionary journey (see map for review, Acts 20:13-37), Paul stops in Miletus (near Ephesus) and asks the elders of the Ephesus church to come see him. This is a sad visit because God has revealed to Paul the trouble that lies ahead for him.

Read: Acts 20:22-37

Ask: Does this sound like the same man who was so adamant about persecuting followers of Christ? (No. God has done a major work in his life. He's a changed man with only one goal – to testify to the gospel of God's grace.)

Ask: Why is Paul so concerned about this church? (He fears that Satan will attack the new church, leading the flock astray. His charge is to be on guard and he prays for these new believers)

Note to Leaders: Stop here and cover Paul's letter to the Romans. He will eventually get to Rome on his forth journey.

In Jerusalem (Act. 21) word has gotten back to the Jewish leaders about Paul's ministry to the Gentiles and, although he presents himself in the temple and makes a public offering, these Jews stir up controversy among the people (much like they did with Christ before the crucifixion). Starting a riot, the whole city seems to turn against Paul, beating and trying to kill him. The Roman solders stop the crowd and arrest Paul. While they're hauling him away to jail the crowd cries, "Away with him." He asks permission to speak to the crowd, and they listen for a moment while he gives a testimony about his conversion (Act. 22:1-21). But then Paul said the Lord told him to go to the Gentiles, and with this the highly prejudiced Jewish crowd goes crazy.

Read: Acts 22:22-29

Ask: What appeal does Paul use to stop the Roman solders from beating him? (He's a Roman citizen and it was illegal to flog a Roman without a trial).

Instructor Notes:

Lesson 10 - Paul's Journeys (cont.)

Acts 23 records the Roman commander's hearing of Paul's case. The Sanhedrin and chief priests gather to accuse Paul, and Paul argues that the only reason he's being mistreated is because he believes in the resurrection of the dead. Since the Pharisees and Sadducees were already divided about this subject, the Roman commander decides to wash his hands of the matter and send Paul on to the governor for a decision.

Paul hears of a plot to kill him while he's being transferred to Caesarea (near the sea, see map), and makes sure the commander is aware of the danger. The commander decides to send Paul immediately, that same night, to Governor Felix.

Acts 24 records Paul's trial before Felix. Felix listens carefully, but unable to make a decision (and hoping that Paul will offer him a bribe), Paul sits in prison for two years. Then Festus replaces Felix and decides to hear Paul's case. His decision is to send Paul on to Caesar. Not wanting to make a mistake, Festus asks the visiting King Agrippa to hear Paul's story, and in the process King Agrippa is nearly convinced to become a Christian. He decides that Paul isn't doing anything wrong, but because Paul has appealed to Caesar he must be sent to Rome for a trial.

Paul's Fourth Journey

In Acts 27 Paul sails for Rome, but on the way a storm causes the ship to run aground. On the island of Malta (Acts 28) Paul is bitten by a poisonous snake, but it has no affect on him. He heals many of the islanders and is treated like royalty. After three months the group set sail for Rome. Once in Rome, Paul is given a relatively high degree of freedom, for a prisoner.

For two years Paul stayed in his own rented house with a soldier to guard him. During this time he wrote Philippians, Colossians, Ephesians and Philemon (read these for next week). Acts stops here, but we know from other writings that Paul is eventually freed, makes other missionary journeys (one to Spain), and eventually ends up back in a Roman prison -- this time for good. The Romans, under Nero (64 AD), turn against Christians and begin the famous habit of feeding them to the lions, throwing them in the arena with Gladiators for entertainment, and burning them on poles to light the emperor's garden. Tradition has it that Paul was killed in Rome for his faith.

Conclusion

The early church owes much of its growth to Paul and other missionaries like him, who boldly preached despite great persecution and at a tremendous personal cost. What does it cost us to be a Christian? You'd think it was easy in today's "whatever you wanna' believe is fine with me" culture. But Christianity is costly. Sometimes is separates families, sometimes it costs the believer friendships, jobs, and choices that could lead to riches. Think about

Instructor Notes:

Lesson 10 - Paul's Journeys (cont.)

the price that was paid so that you could hear and receive the gospel, then think about what you're doing to carry the faith to others. Consider how willing you are to pay the price that faith in Christ may cost you.

Questions?

For Next Week:
Next week we will cover the letters of Paul. Read as many as you can.

Close in prayer.

Instructor Notes:

_____
_____
_____
_____
_____
_____
_____
_____
_____
_____
_____

Basic Bible 101 - The New Testament
Lesson 11 - Paul's Letters

Preparing for the class: *Your students will not be able to absorb all that you cover in this lesson, but they will get a taste of Paul's writings. The goal is to encourage your students to return to the passages you introduce at a later date and study them individually. It is crucial that you spend time reading the target passages and the introductions to each of the books covered. Think through what you will say about each book so that your summary will be accurate and brief. It is important to realize that Paul's letters reflect his beliefs. They are personal thoughts communicated to people he loved. As you present the lesson remember you are introducing your students to a man (just an ordinary man) who allowed the spirit of God to change the world through him. His words are just as powerful today as they were then because they were inspired by the Holy Spirit.*

Presenting the lesson: Read as much of Paul's letters as possible. Specifically read the introduction to the following books: Romans, 1&2 Corinthians, Galatians, Ephesians, Philippians, Colossians, 1&2 Thessalonians, 1&2 Timothy, Titus, Philemon. Also read these passages: Romans Road to Salvation (Romans 3:23; 6:23, 5:8, 10:9-10;13); Doctrinal passages in Romans: 7:14-25, 8:1; 9:16; 8:26-39; 12:1-2; 1 Cor: 6:12-20; 13; 2 Cor. 4, 5:17; Galatians: 1, 2, 3:1-5, 28; 5:1, 13-14, 22; 6:7-10; Ephesians: 2:8; 4:1+; 5:8, 15-22; All of chpt 6 Philippians: 2:12-17; 3, 4:4-9; Colossians: 1:10, 2:6-10; 3:12-17; 4:2-6; 1 Thes: 2:1-13, 4:11-18; 5+; 1 Tim. 1:2-16; 2 Tim. 3:16

Paul's letters are loosely grouped here by common themes and target audiences. Paul frequently wrote the same thing to more than one church, probably because the same problems cropped up in more than one place. Use the passages as a springboard for discussion of the major themes in Paul's letters (i.e. grace vs. works, remaining faithful despite persecution, our worth in Christ, rejecting false teachings, getting along with each other as the body of Christ).

Opening: Last week we walked in the steps of Paul as he traveled through Galatia, Macedonia and Greece, first with Barnabus, then with Silas. In each place Paul managed to gain more converts through his persistent attempts to understand and relate to the local populous. He was persecuted, stoned, imprisoned, whipped, ship wrecked, bit by a snake, tried in various courts and eventually killed for his beliefs.

Ask: Why was Paul willing to endure all this hardship? (Before anyone answers have them read the next passage – Paul's only motivation is to live up to the calling he has received.)

Read: 1 Timothy 1:12-16 and 1 Thes. 2:1-13

Ask: Who is Paul seeking to please? (God).

In this passage we get a glimpse of the way Paul dealt with new believers. He describes himself as a "mother" and a "father" caring,

Instructor Notes:

_____
_____
_____
_____
_____
_____
_____
_____
_____
_____
_____

encouraging and comforting his children. These same attributes are evident in the letters he wrote back to the churches he began. Notice the personal tone he takes in each letter and the specific problem he addresses. Let's begin with Romans.

Romans - It is believed that Paul wrote the book of Romans while at Corinth during his third missionary journey (apx.57 BC). Paul anticipated visiting the Christians in Rome and sent this letter to explain his understanding of the doctrine of Christianity. Paul explains how all have sinned and need God's forgiveness, and how Christ is the only way to obtain that forgiveness. He addresses our struggles with a sinful nature, and reminds us that our salvation is dependent on faith alone. He reminds us not to be a stumbling block for our brothers and sisters in Christ. In this book is a simple presentation of the gospel, often referred to as the "Romans Road to Salvation." Let's look at some of these passages:

Read: Romans 3:23 (All have sinned); 6:23 (The wages of sin is death), 5:8 (Christ died to pay our sin debt), 10:9-10;13 (Confess Jesus and you will be saved). Invite your students to memorize these verses.

Other great passages in this book are: Roman 7:14-2 (our struggle with sin), 8:1; 9:16 (the victory against sin is not based on our strength); 8:26-39 (we are conquerors in Christ); 12:1-2 (we are to present ourselves a living sacrifice). Point out any other favorite passages you find in Romans. The book of Romans is a great place for new Christians to discover what we believe and why.

Galatians – Possibly Paul's first letter, this book was written to the churches of Galatia after Paul returned from his first missionary journey. Here he counters some popular myths being circulated at that time, namely that Christians had to become Jews. Paul clearly states GRACE is our claim to godliness, and nothing else. Only by Christ's death are we considered worthy of God's love and forgiveness, and it is that GRACE that keeps us walking day by day in step with the Holy Spirit. Some interesting facts about how Paul learned so much about Jesus, and the timetable in which all these events took place, is explained in chapter 1:15 through 2:1. Paul takes on Peter, the head of the church in Jerusalem, clearly stating that the Gentile converts did not have to follow the old Jewish laws. Chapter 5 reminds us of our freedom in Christ. The last part of chapter 5 talks about the fruit of the spirit, qualities that grow within us as we grow in Christ.

1 Corinthians – The first letter written to the Corinthians, Paul wrote this letter to the church in Greece while he was in Ephesus during his third missionary journey. This letter was written to help the believers understand how to live for Christ in a pagan society. If you remember, Corinth was a major hub at the crossroads of the known world. The popular philosophy of the people then was "anything goes." Much like our society today, sin was a relative issue and everyone

Instructor Notes:

Lesson 11 - Paul's Letters

felt justified in making up their own rules of conduct. The church was heavily influenced by the carnal tendencies of society. Paul urges the believers there to settle their disputes and stop arguing over petty matters. He wanted them to grow up in their faith, stop tolerating sexual misconduct, and test every teaching they hear. 1 Corinthians contains the Love Chapter (1 Cor. 13) and some specific instructions for marriage and the role of women, as well as guidelines for using spiritual gifts such as speaking in tongues. Check out these passages:

Read: 1 Cor: 6:12-20; 13:1-13

2 Corinthians – It is believed that 2 Corinthians was actually the third letter to this church in Greece. Because the controversies in the church were causing some to doubt Paul's apostleship credentials, he defends his call from God at length. He reminds these believers that our competency comes from God. He writes about the Holy Spirit and how it is our assurance (guarantee) of what is to come – eternal life. He explains how God turns our weakness into strength. Again here he lashes out against false teachers. A favorite passage is in Chapter 4 where Paul describes how the glory of God is in us, as in jars of clay. It's not the jar that's precious, but what's inside. 2 Corinthians is filled with images of who we are in Christ.

Read: 2 Cor. 4:7-18 and 2 Cor. 5:17

1 Thessalonians - Both 1 & 2 Thessalonians were letters written to the church at Thessalonica, which Paul founded but was forced to leave after only three weeks on his first journey. Here he encourages the new believers and is delighted to see that they are progressing in their faith. He cautions them about sexual misconduct and explains some interesting insights on what happens when Christians die. He emphasizes that Christ will return soon.

Read: 1 Thes: 4:11-18

2 Thessalonians - A follow-up letter to 1 Thessalonians, this letter deals with some possible misunderstandings resulting from his first letter. He encourages the believers to hold firm during persecution, and then corrects their mistaken idea that because Christ is coming soon they should all just be idle while looking up to the sky for his return. He says anyone that won't work won't eat.

The next four books were written during Paul's first imprisonment in Rome.

Ephesians - Paul wrote this letter to the church at Ephesus to express God's plan for a new society. He explains how God chose us before we chose him, and how we are to live in peace with one another. He gives some guidelines for using our special gifts to help the entire body of Christ, the church. The last chapter, sometimes referred to as the "armor of God" chapter, explains how to prepare for battle

Instructor Notes:

against evil. Here are some key passages to consider:

Read: Ephesians: 2:8; 4:1-6; 5:8, 15-25; 6:10-19

Philippians – This letter to the church at Philippi is written in a very tender style. Paul writes to thank the church for supporting him, and rejoices in all that God is doing. An optimistic letter, Philippians encourages gratitude, despite suffering, and remaining faithful in the hope that God will use every circumstance for good.

Read: Philippians: 2:12-17; 3, 4:4-9

Colossians – Paul wrote this letter to the church in Colossae even though it is unlikely that Paul ever visited there. Rather, this church was probably a mission of the church in Ephesus. He emphasizes the fullness and freedom we have in Christ. To counter some false teaching he warns them not to be misled, there is only one way to heaven and that is through Jesus Christ. Much like he does in the book of Galatians, Paul warns not to let the legalism fanatics enslave them, but to live for Christ

Read: Colossians: 1:10; 2:6-12; 3:12-25

Philemon – In this letter to Philemon, Paul urges him to accept and forgive his runaway slave, Onesimus, who is a fellow Christian. This letter sets the standard for treating everyone in Christ as a brother (no more second class citizens).

These final letters of Paul were written to his proteges (two men he groomed for ministry).

Titus – This letter to Titus, one of Paul's faithful companions, was written to help Titus set up a new church with proper leadership and oneness. He includes rules for elders, and encourages the people to be subject to their authority. He sets up standards that say "No" to ungodliness.

1 Timothy – In this first letter to his dear friend, Timothy, Paul repeats some of the counsel he gave to Titus, but the slant is different because Timothy is working with an established, but wayward church. He gives instructions for worship, pastors, deacons, widows, and slaves. He warns against false teachers and tells them to guard against the love of money.

Read: 1 Tim. 3:1-7

2 Timothy – This is Paul's last letter and it is written while he is in prison awaiting his death. Here Paul once more reminds Timothy to remain faithful, to pass on the faith, and to expect persecution. He tells him to always be prepared to preach, and to preach the truth. He assures Timothy that he (Paul) is prepared for eternity. He asks

Instructor Notes:

Lesson 11 - Paul's Letters

Timothy to bring him his winter coat. Paul was killed shortly after this letter was written.

Read: 2 Tim. 3:16, 4:6-13

Conclusion:

1. Only God's grace can bring about God's righteousness in us.
2. Expect persecution, but know that God will use it for our good.
3. Paul was practical and culturally relevant in his instructions to the early churches.
4. Paul's letters are an excellent source of wisdom for sorting out what you believe.

Next Week: For next week read as much as you can of Hebrews, James, 1&2 Peter, 1-3 John, Jude

Prayer requests.

Close in prayer.

Instructor Notes:

Basic Bible 101 - The New Testament
Lesson 12 - The Other Letters

Preparing for the class: *Spend some time reading the books to be presented today (Hebrews, James, 1&2 Peter, 1-3 John, Jude). Be sure to review the introductions to each book. You are nearing the end of this course so pass out the New Testament final review and spend a few moments reminding your students of what you've already covered in the New Testament (the Gospels, Acts, Paul's Journeys, Paul's Letters). Pass out Quiz 2 and give everyone a chance to think about the answers. Then go over the answers together. Set out the coffee/juice/snacks or whatever refreshments you decide to serve. Greet students as they arrive.*

Presenting the lesson: Start out today's lesson with a short review of Paul's letters. Transition to a short introduction of today's letter writers – Peter, James, John and Jude. Point out that the author of Hebrews is unknown.

Opening: Last week we covered the letters Paul wrote to the early churches in Ephesus, Corinth, Greece and so forth. Today we will look at the letters written by other apostles. But first let's look at the book of Hebrews.

Hebrews

We really don't know who wrote this letter, but it is written to Jewish Christians who were trying to understand how to fit their new faith in Jesus into their old religion. It is possible that Paul either wrote this letter or dictated the letter to one of his assistants because it is filled with doctrine. The author is well versed in Jewish beliefs and clearly explains how Jesus is our new High Priest. This book explains how Jesus is superior to angels and the Old Testament prophets. It reminds these Jewish believers to stay firm in the faith in spite of tremendous persecution. Jewish families rejected family members who because Christians. They wouldn't even look at them or allow them in their home. In the book of Hebrews is what some have called "The Hall of Fame" for the faithful. Let's look at it.

Read: Hebrews 11:1-32

Ask: How does the author show that faith was a pre-requisite for a right relationship with God even in the Old Testament? (he gives examples of individuals who listened to God and acted on God's promises).

James

Now let's turn to the letter written by James, the brother of Jesus. This book has an entirely different sound. James begins by encouraging the believers to endure hardships with faith because these earthly struggles build up our faith. He chastises wealthy believers to give to those in need. His letter is filled with the call to live out our faith through good works. You might say this book is the counterpoint to Galatians. Galatians stressed that works were

Instructor Notes:

_____
_____
_____
_____
_____
_____
_____
_____
_____
_____
_____
_____

Lesson 12 - The Other Letters

nothing. We are saved by grace. But James clearly explains that faith is always accompanied by good works. We live out our faith through lives changed by the gospel of Christ. Our new life in Christ is one characterized by good works.

Read: James 1:22-25

Ask: What does James ask believers to be? (doers of the Word, not just hearers)

1 Peter

Peter was the leader of the early church. As you know he had his differences with Paul, but it is clear from his letters that he is a gentle man with sincere love for his brothers and sisters in the faith. His first letter is written to persecuted believers, encouraging them to hold firm to their faith despite suffering and rejection. He reminds them that the suffering we endure on earth is temporary, but our rewards in heaven are eternal. He advises women who are married to unbelievers to be submissive to their husband, not arguing with them over their new faith. Instead, to let the unbelieving husband see what a difference faith makes and perhaps be persuaded to accept Christ through their wife's gentle influence.

Read: 1 Peter 2:11-21

Ask: Who does Peter say we should be submissive to and why? (all authorities so that they may see Christ in us).

2 Peter

In this second letter written by Peter he warns strongly against false teachers. One of the ways enemies of Christians would attack the church is by causing disagreements among Christians. If they could break up the believers perhaps the movement would die. Peter warns that if not even the angels were spared when they sinned God will certainly bring to judgement these false teachers. Peter also encourages the believers to live holy lives, worthy of the call they have received.

Read: 2 Peter 2:1-4

Ask: What do false teachers really want from us? (money)

1 John

The apostle John (the one who wrote the book of John) wrote these three letters later in his ministry. He also wrote the book of Revelations which we will cover in our next lesson. In his first letter he seeks to promote unity among the believers. This letter begins in a very similar way to the book of John, focusing on who Jesus was and why he came. He reminds the believers that if we confess our sins Jesus is faithful to forgive us and cleanse us from all unrighteousness (1 John 1:9). Like a wise old grandfather, John encourages the

Instructor Notes:

Lesson 12 - The Other Letters

believers to love one another. To avoid false teachers and to live out their faith to the end.

2 John
In this second letter John is arguing against a popular myth that Jesus wasn't really human. He clearly states that Jesus was human. As one who lived with Jesus, he could testify to this fact. He watched Jesus die. John wanted to discuss this personally with those who were being led astray so this letter is really just an introduction to the topic they would later discuss in more depth in person.

3 John
Here John encourages believers to support one another in service for the sake of Christ. He reproofs Diotrephes (apparently one who is speaking against John) and commends Demetrius as someone worth following. Again, John likes to discuss issues in person so he cuts this letter short as well.

Jude
The last letter we will consider today was written by Jude, probably a younger brother of James. He is also writing to counter false teachings. He encourages believers to defend the gospel and demonstrate its power by living godly lives. He condemns the false teachers who are destroying the faith of some. But he reminds the believers that Jesus is able to keep them in the faith.

Read: Jude 1:24-25

Ask: How will Jesus present us to the Lord on judgement day? (without spot or blemish – perfect).

Conclusion:

1. False teachers were trying to destroy the early church so the early church leaders sent letters of encouragement to the persecuted believers.
2. The letter of James commends proving our faith by our works – quite a different emphasis than Galatians which proclaims grace alone for righteousness.
3. Peter and John both encourage living in unity, loving one another and remaining faithful to the end despite persecution.

Questions?

Next Week: For next week read the last book of the Bible - Revelation.

Prayer requests.

Close in prayer.

Instructor Notes:

Basic Bible 101 - The New Testament
Lesson 13 - Revelations

Preparing for the class: *Finish your reading of Revelations. This is a controversial book because so much of it is symbolic and/or futuristic. You may want to glance through some commentaries of Revelations, but with so many different opinions the best approach is just to introduce your students to the content. Future Bible studies can then deal with the interpretation. Set out the coffee/juice/snacks or whatever refreshments you decide to serve. Greet students as they arrive.*

Presenting the lesson: If possible hang or copy a map showing the location of the early churches in Asia. *Nelson's Complete Book of Bible Maps and Charts* has a clear, simple map of this area with the location of each church marked.

Opening: Last week we covered the letters written by someone other than Paul. Today we will cover the last book of the New Testament, Revelations. Revelations starts out like a letter from John, but quickly turns into a detailed vision he had. This vision occurred while John was exiled on the island of Patmos. Because the Christian community was greatly persecuted at that time much of the communication between churches is written in code with language known to early Christians, but not easily understood by outsiders. That's why some of this may be difficult for us to understand. The first three chapters John is writing directly to the main churches in Asia. Let's look at what John is saying to each one.

John describes in chapter one his vision of a man who obviously reminds him of Jesus except that he is as white as snow with fiery eyes. This man tells him to write down what he sees, what is now and what will later be. He explains that the seven lampstands John saw represent the seven churches, and that the seven stars in the man's hands represent the seven angels of these churches. From here on John writes a specific message to each "angel" or messenger.

Read: Rev. 2:1-7

Ask: What is message to the church in Ephesus? (You reject evil and endure trials patiently, but your love for Christ wanes. Do the works you did at first).

To the church in Ephesus he includes both a word of praise, and a concern to be addressed. He mentions his condemnation of the "Nicolaitans," which at that time were false teachers trying to lead new believers astray. The term is likely derived from Balaam's sin, which was to convince the people to turn to idol worship (those who took the Old Testament class will remember that Balaam was the one with the talking donkey in Numbers 22). This sin is mentioned in Numbers 31:16. The church in Ephesus is challenged to return to the devotion for Christ they had at the beginning or face having their "lampstand removed." Obedience would be rewarded with eternal life.

Instructor Notes:

Read: Rev. 2:8-11

Ask: What was the message to the church in Smyrna? (you are rich despite your poverty. Trials are coming - stay true to the end)

The church in Smyrna is already suffering, but the message to this church encourages them to hang in there, even to the point of death. A crown of life awaits them.

Read: Rev. 2:12-17

Ask: What was the message to the church in Pergamum? (although you hold true to Christ you are putting up with false teachers in your midst. Repent or face the consequences)

Although they live in the very heart of a wicked city, the church in Pergamum had remained true to their faith. Again, this church is dealing with false teachers, "Nicolaitans," who are misleading believers. They must be dealt with or the entire church will answer for it.

Read: Rev. 2:18-20

Ask: What was the message to the church in Thyatira? (This church is doing more than at first, but are being tolerant of an immoral woman leading the flock astray).

It's obvious the churches are being infiltrated by people trying to corrupt the faith of the believers. False teachings abound. Even once strong Christians are becoming complacent.

The church in Sardis is accused of being dead (Rev. 3:1-6) and the church in Laodicea is neither hot nor cold, in need of repentance because they are blind to their own condition. These are sad reports for churches that were once so excited to share the gospel. The church in Philadelphia received a good report. They have been faithful to proclaim Christ and because of this will avoid the coming tribulation.

Let's talk for a minute about this tribulation. From chapter four through the end of the book John describes a scene in heaven. John first describes a throne with someone sitting on. This person on the throne was flashing brilliant colors of light, like jewels. Around him were 24 thrones each occupied by an elder. Then he describes other beings, spirits, creatures, things that were very strange to him. Everything was giving glory and praise to the One on the throne. Bible scholars have studied these passages and have reached various conclusions. It is difficult to just read this book because the story just gets more bizarre. Chapter five describes a scroll which is sealed with seven seals. The only one worthy to open the scroll is the lamb that was slain. At this point you are probably concluding that

Instructor Notes:

Lesson 13 - Revelations

Instructor Notes:

_____
_____
_____
_____
_____
_____
_____
_____
_____
_____
_____

these images are symbolic, and that the lamb must be Jesus Christ. What we don't know is whether the events John is describing are purely symbolic, depicting the struggle between good and evil in the spiritual realm, or if the symbols represent actual events to come. Even those who believe the images are prophetic disagree over when the events will happen, or even if they've already happened since that first century. We could spend weeks covering all the symbols, their probably meaning, and how we should apply these meanings to our lives. For today we will just cover the main events in John's vision, and the most common interpretations of these events.

As the lamb begins to open the scroll each seal he breaks unleashes a horseman who rides throughout the land. The first is to conquer, the second to take away peace, the third to wreak economical havoc. The fourth horseman brings death to a fourth of the land. The fifth seal presents a crowd of people who have suffered for the word of God. They are given a white robe and told to wait a little longer. The sixth seal unleashed a great earthquake that caused mass destruction throughout the earth. At this point all the inhabitants of earth wish they were dead because they are so afraid of the wrath of the "lamb." An angel says "wait" so that all the servants of God still on earth can be marked with God's seal on their forehead. The number is 144,000.

You can see why these images are so hard to interpret. Are they part of the tribulation that John eludes to in chapter 3, or are they images of the end of the world? Is the number 144,000 literal or just representative of the remaining believers on the earth? Are they Christians? John proceeds to count 12,000 for each of the 12 tribes of Israel so perhaps they are Jews. He then describes a large multitude of people too many to count who have been delivered out of the great tribulation. They have "washed their robes and made them white in the blood of the Lamb." Sounds like believers to me, but are they believers who have died, or were they mysteriously removed from the earth? This is where we get references to the "rapture," the day when all believers just disappear from earth.

As the seventh seal is broken seven angels appear, each with a trumpet. As each angel blows the trumpet given them unpleasant things happen on earth. A third of the earth is burned up, a third of the sea turns to blood, a third of the rivers are poisoned and a third of the sun is blocked along with a third of the moon and stars. More pain and suffering come to the inhabitants of the earth with the blowing of the other trumpets until the earth is declared the kingdom of the Lord.

In chapter 11 John talks about two witnesses who preach repentance for three and a half years. They are killed, but after three days they come back to life and ascend into heaven on a cloud. Chapters 12 through 13 describes a battle between a woman and a dragon, then the arrival of the "anti-Christ" bearing the number 666. The war, which is termed "Armageddon" rages on until the end of Revelations when Christ reigns for 1000 years. After that the dead are judged and a new heaven and earth are created for all God's people.

The *Left Behind* series of books by Tim LaHaye and Jerry Jenkins are based on events from Revelations, but keep in mind their's is just one interpretation of John's vision. Bible scholars differ greatly on the interpretation of this book. You may hear church people talk about "pre-tribuation" versus "post-tribulation," or "premillennial" versus "post-millennial" views. These arguments are interesting to consider, but it is pointless to argue over what we cannot know for certain. It is very likely that even John didn't understand the vision.

Revelations presents more questions than answers, but it is an interesting book to study because some of the events described do sound a lot like what's happening in our world today. Christians have waited over 2000 years for Christ to return to earth. When you study Revelations you realize that the time could be drawing near. Jesus says in Revelations 22:7 "Behold, I am coming soon! Blessed is he who keeps the words of the prophecy in this book." That leads me to believe it is wise to study this mysterious book, but we won't really understand it all until Christ explains it to us in person. One more point about this book. Look at the very end of Revelations.

Read: Rev. 22:18-21

Ask: What is the warning here? (not to add to or subtract from the words of this book)

This warning reminds us that John had the task of writing the final words of scripture. Anyone who states there are other revelations from God that should be included, additional books or missing scriptures, is treading some dangerous ground.

Conclusion:

1. The first few chapters of Revelations include praise and warnings for the churches. Some of these same concerns can be applied to churches today.
2. John's vision is symbolic, explaining events in heaven that he saw happen in his vision. When they will happen, or even if they have happened, is up to interpretation.
3. No one should add to or take away from the Bible. Anyone who does should be considered a false teacher.

Next Week: Review for the final. A review sheet can be found on the Basicbible101.com website in the student section.

Prayer requests. Close in prayer.

Instructor Notes:

Quiz 1 - The Life of Jesus

1. How did Mary know the child she was carrying was the son of God? _____

2. Who did God send to "prepare the way" for Jesus by preaching repentance and baptizing people?
_____

3. Why did Mary and Joseph travel to Bethlehem before the baby was born? _____

4. When Jesus went into the wilderness alone for 40 days what happened to him?
_____

5. Name as many of the disciples (12 apostles) as you can:
_____
_____
_____

6. What did Jesus promise to give the Samaratan woman at the well?
_____

7. What is your favorite parable and why?
_____
_____

8. List some of the miracles Jesus did?
_____
_____

9. Which disciple grabbed a sword and lopped off the ear of a soldier when they came to capture Jesus?
_____

10. Why did Jesus have to die?
_____
_____
_____

Quiz 2 - Paul

1. What was Paul's name and occupation before he became a believer?

   _____

2. Why didn't the other believers accept Paul right away?

   _____

   _____

3. Who stood up for Paul and encouraged him in his new faith?

   _____

4. Where did Paul go on his first missionary journey?

   _____

5. Who went with Paul on the first journey? the second journey?

   _____

   _____

6. Which of Paul's letters centers on GRACE, the fact that we can do nothing to earn our salvation?

   _____

7. Which of Paul's letters was written to a church he had never visited?

   _____

8. Where's the last place we find Paul in the New Testament?

   _____

New Testament Final

Match the names listed with the statements below.

a. Timothy
b. Peter
c. Matthew
d. John
e. Barnabus

f. Luke
g. Saul
h. Mary
i. Judas
j. Stephen

_____ 1. He traveled with Paul and wrote one of the gospels and the book of Acts.

_____ 2. The Sermon on the Mount is found in this first book of the New Testament.

_____ 3. She was a virgin when an angel told her she was going to have a son.

_____ 4. He betrayed Jesus with a kiss.

_____ 5. He preached a powerful sermon on the day of Pentecost when 3000 people were saved. He also wrote two books of the Bible.

_____ 6. This martyr was killed by stoning for his beliefs about Jesus.

_____ 7. He encountered Jesus on the Road to Damascus and was blinded for three days.

_____ 8. He is known as the "Son of Encouragement" because he stood up for Paul. He traveled with Paul on his first missionary journey.

_____ 9. Paul wrote his last few letters to this dear "son" as advice to a young pastor. This man also traveled with him on his second journey.

_____ 10. He refers to himself as the "disciple whom Jesus loved." He wrote one gospel, several letters and the last book in the Bible.

Choose the ONE best answer to complete each of the following statements.

11. Paul wrote these two letters to a church in Greece which struggled with worldliness. Paul encouraged them to live for Christ in a pagan society. The Love chapter is also in one of these books. They are:

    a. 1 & 2 Snuffulufugus
    b. 1 & 2 Peter
    c. 1 & 2 Timothy
    d. 1 & 2 Corinthians

12. In one of Paul's best books on DOCTRINE he wrote to the Christians living in a city to which he had not yet been, but intended to visit. This letter is the book of:

    a. Romans
    b. Spaniards
    c. Galatians
    d. Jude

13. This book is one of Paul's first letters and strongly supports Paul's view of GRACE, not works, as the basis for salvation. Written to the Christians he visited on his first journey, this books is:

    a. Philippians
    b. Galatians
    c. Colossians
    d. Ephesians

14. Paul wrote this book to persuade a slave owner to forgive his runaway slave, Onesimus.

    a. Titus
    b. Philemon
    c. Jude
    d. James

15. This book was written by one of the early church elders, the brother of Jesus, who strongly believed in WORKS as the proof of one's faith. This book is:

    a. Hebrews
    b. James
    c. Revelations
    d. 3 John

16. This book, written by an apostle, is the record of a vision he received about the future, some of which has yet to come about. This is the book of:

    a. 1 John
    b. Hebrews
    c. Ephesians
    d. Revelations

17. Paul wrote three of the following books while he was in prison awaiting his opportunity to plead his case before Caesar. Which book is not a "prison epistle":

    a. Colossians
    b. Hebrews
    c. Philippians
    d. Titus

18. These two books, written by the leader of the early church, encourage believers to hang in there during persecution and resist false teachers. They are:

    a. 1 & 2 Thessalonians
    b. 1 & 2 Peter
    c. 1 & 2 John
    d. 1 & 2 Corinthians

You're doing great – keep going!

Match the places listed with the statements below.

a. Golgatha
b. Bethany
c. Sea of Galilee
d. Galilee
e. Wilderness
f. Samaria
g. Jerusalem
h. Bethlehem
i. Nazareth
j. Egypt

____ 19. Jesus was born here.

____ 20. Jesus was raised and rejected here.

____ 21. Jesus began his ministry in this area and preached the Sermon on the Mount here.

____ 22. Jesus walked on the water here.

____ 23. Jesus was tempted here.

____ 24. Jesus was taken here to avoid Herod's death sentance on all babies two and under.

____ 25. Jesus raised his friend Lazarus from the dead here.

____ 26. Jesus was crucified here.

____ 27. Jesus spoke to the woman at the well here.

____ 28. Jesus entered this city triumphantly on Palm Sunday, one week before his crucifixion.

29. What must we do to be saved?

Extra Credit:

1 Point for each disciple you can name:

Congratulations on completing Basic Bible 101 The New Testament!

BASIC BIBLE 101 ASSESSMENT TEST – NEW TESTAMENT

Name:_____

Match the names on the left with the statements on the right.

____ 1. He was one of Jesus' followers, wrote one of the gospels and the book of Acts.
____ 2. The Sermon on the Mount is found in this first book of the New Testament.
____ 3. She was a virgin when an angel told her she was going to have a son.
____ 4. He betrayed Jesus with a kiss.
____ 5. He preached a powerful sermon on the day of Pentecost when 3000 people were saved. He also wrote 2 books of the Bible.
____ 6. He was stoned for his strong beliefs about Jesus.
____ 7. He encountered Jesus on the Road to Damascus and was blind for 3 days.
____ 8. He is known as the "Son of Encouragement" because he stood up for Paul. He traveled with Paul on his first missionary journey.
____ 9. Paul wrote his last few letters to this dear "son" as advice to a young pastor. This man also traveled with him on his second missionary journey.
____10. He refers to himself as the "disciple whom Jesus loved." He wrote one gospel, several letters and the last book in the Bible.

a. Timothy
b. Peter
c. Matthew
d. John
e. Barnabus
f. Luke
g. Saul
h. Mary
i. Judas
j. Stephen

BASIC BIBLE 101 ASSESSMENT TEST – NEW TESTAMENT

Match the names on the left with the statements on the right.

Name:_____

____ 1. He was one of Jesus' followers, wrote one of the gospels and the book of Acts.
____ 2. The Sermon on the Mount is found in this first book of the New Testament.
____ 3. She was a virgin when an angel told her she was going to have a son.
____ 4. He betrayed Jesus with a kiss.
____ 5. He preached a powerful sermon on the day of Pentecost when 3000 people were saved. He also wrote 2 books of the Bible.
____ 6. He was stoned for his strong beliefs about Jesus.
____ 7. He encountered Jesus on the Road to Damascus and was blind for 3 days.
____ 8. He is known as the "Son of Encouragement" because he stood up for Paul. He traveled with Paul on his first missionary journey.
____ 9. Paul wrote his last few letters to this dear "son" as advice to a young pastor. This man also traveled with him on his second missionary journey.
____10. He refers to himself as the "disciple whom Jesus loved." He wrote one gospel, several letters and the last book in the Bible

a. Timothy
b. Peter
c. Matthew
d. John
e. Barnabus
f. Luke
g. Saul
h. Mary
i. Judas
j. Stephen

Answers to Quizzes & Final

Quiz 1 - The Life of Jesus

1. An angel told her.
2. John the Baptist.
3. Because a census was decreed by King Herod and they had to go to their birthplace to register.
4. He was tempted by Satan.
5. Disciples: John, James, Andrew, (Simon) Peter, Simon (the zealot), Bartholomew, Philip, Thomas, Thaddaeus (aka Judas son of James), Matthew, James (son of Alphaeus), Judas Iscariot
6. Jesus promised to give her living water so she would never thurst again.
7. Any will do as long as it really was a parable Jesus told.
8. Any will do as long as it is recorded in the Bible.
9. Peter
10. So that the debt for our sins would be paid.

Quiz 2 - Paul

1. Paul was Saul, a tentmaker and Pharasee.
2. Because Saul had been persecuting the early believers, stoning them and throwing them in prison.
3. Barnabus (Ananias could be mentioned here as well)
4. Into modern day Turkey, Galatia or any of the cities mentioned in the lesson on Paul's first journey.
5. First journey: Barnabus   Second journey: Silas, Timothy & Luke
6. Galatians
7. Colossians, although this can be disputed.
8. Under house arrest in Rome.

Final Exam

1. f	2. c	3. h	4. i	5. b	6. j	7. g	8. e	9. a	10. d
11. d	12. a	13. b	14. b	15. b	16. d	17. b	18. b	19. h	20. i
21. d	22. c	23. e	24. j	25. b	26. a	27. f	28. g		

29. Believe in your heart and profess with your mouth that Jesus is Lord.

Disciples:
John, James, Andrew, (Simon) Peter, Simon (the zealot), Bartholomew, Philip, Thomas, Thaddaeus (aka Judas son of James), Matthew, James (son of Alphaeus), Judas Iscariot

About the Author

Raised in a relatively conservative Christian home, Margie Smith found the truths of Christ easy to accept. As a youth she personalized these truths and was baptized, joining a Southern Baptist Church in Spokane, Washington. In college she and her husband Brian attended a rather unconventional Free Evangelical church, attending a weekly couples Bible study and working in the Baptist Student Ministries on campus.

In 1987 Margie and Brian moved to Dallas, Texas with their two children. Margie has been a life-long student of the Bible, teaching various children and adult Bible classes along the way. She has served as both a Small Group Leader and Coach. Margie is currently a member of Woodcreek Church, Richardson Texas. Additionally, she owns a Dallas-based advertising agency.

Margie has always enjoyed working with new believers. She developed the Basic Bible 101 curriculum as a way to bridge the gap when adults become believers in Christ and attempt to understand the Bible for the first time in their lives.

Answers to the Homework and Lesson Notes
Answers to the questions posed in the homework and lesson notes can be found online at http://www.basicbible101.com under the Lesson Notes heading.

Quizzes, Handouts, Review Sheets and The Final Exam
To access the quizzes, handouts, review sheets and the final exam, log into the student area of the website using **student** as the username and **basicbible101** as the password. Group leaders can find more information in the leaders section of the website: username **leader** and password **bible101.**

How to Order More Workbooks
Basic Bible 101 Old Testament student workbooks can be purchased online through the Basic Bible 101 website (http://www.basicbible101.com) or on Amazon. You can write to:

Basic Bible 101
c/o Margie Smith
PO Box 941843
Plano, TX 75094

Email: margie@basicbible101.com

An Old Testament version of this course is also available.

Basic Bible 101 © 2003 Margaret A. Smith www.basicbible101.com